FLASHMAPS
NEW YORK

W9-CEP-819

Editorial Updater
Martha Schulman

Cartographic Updater
Marcy Pritchard

Proofreader
Susan Ryan

Editor
Robert Blake

Cover Design
Guido Caroti

Creative Director
Fabrizio La Rocca

Cartographer
David Lindroth

Designer
Tigist Getachew

Cartographic Contributors
Edward Faherty
Sheila Levin
Page Lindroth
Eric Rudolph

Contents

Copyright © 2000 by Fodor's Travel Publications

Fodor's Travel Publications is a registered trademark of Random House, Inc. Flashmaps is a registered trademark of Newberry Award Records, Inc.

All rights reserved under International and Pan-American Copyright Conventions. Published in the United States by Fodor's Travel Publications, a division of Random House, Inc., New York, and simultaneously in Canada by Random House of Canada Limited, Toronto. Distributed by Random House, Inc., New York. No maps, illustrations, or other portions of this book may be reproduced in any form without written permission from the publishers. While care has been taken to ensure the accuracy of this guide, information does change, and the publisher cannot accept responsibility for errors that may occur.

Special Sales

Fodor's Travel Publications are available at special discounts for bulk purchases for sales promotions or premiums. Special editions, including personalized covers, excerpts of existing guides, and corporate imprints, can be created in large quantities for special needs. For more information, contact your local bookseller or write to Special Markets, Fodor's Travel Publications, 201 East 50th St., New York, NY 10022. Inquiries from Canada should be directed to your local Canadian bookseller or sent to Random House of Canada, Ltd., Marketing Dept., 2775 Matheson Blvd. East, Mississauga, Ontario L4W4P7. Inquiries from the United Kingdom should be sent to Fodor's Travel Publications, 20 Vauxhall Bridge Rd., London, England SW1V 2SA. **ISBN 0-679-00407-6**

PRINTED IN THE UNITED STATES OF AMERICA 10 9 8 7 6 5 4 3 2 1

Area Codes: Manhattan (212, 646); Bronx, Brooklyn, Queens, Staten Island (718); Nassau/Suffolk (516); Northern NJ (201, 973).
All (212) unless otherwise noted.

EMERGENCIES

AAA Emergency Road Service ☎ 800/222-4357

Ambulance, Fire, Police ☎ 911

Animal Bites ☎ 676-2483

Animal Medical Center ☎ 838-8100

Arson Hotline ☎ 800/FIRE-TIP

Battered Women ☎ 800/942-6906

Child Abuse ☎ 800/342-3720

Crime Victim Hotline ☎ 577-7777

Dental Emergency ☎ 677-2510

Drug Abuse ☎ 800/395-3400

Hospital Patient Location Information ☎ 718/416-7000

Lesbian and Gay Anti-Violence Project ☎ 714-1141

Mental Health Crisis Hotline/LifeNet ☎ 800/543-3638

Park Emergencies ☎ 800/201-7275

Poison Control ☎ 340-4494

Rape Hotline ☎ 800/621-4000

Runaway Hotline ☎ 227-3000

Sex Crimes Reports ☎ 267-7273

Suicide Prevention ☎ 673-3000

SERVICES

AAA ☎ 757-2000

AIDS Hotline (CDC) ☎ 800/342-2437

AIDS Hotline (NYC) ☎ 800/825-5448

Alcoholics Anonymous ☎ 870-3400

Amex Lost Travelers Checks ☎ 800/221-7282

ASPCA ☎ 876-7700

Better Business Bureau ☎ 533-6200

Big Apple Greeters ☎ 669-2896

Chamber of Commerce ☎ 493-7400

Consumer Affairs ☎ 487-4444

Convention & Visitor's Bureau ☎ 397-8222

Department of Aging ☎ 442-1000

Department of Health ☎ 442-9666

Department of Sanitation ☎ 219-8090

Department of Transportation ☎ 768-4653

Gay and Lesbian Hotline ☎ 989-0999

Housing Authority ☎ 306-3000

Immigration/Naturalization ☎ 800/375-5283

Legal Aid Society ☎ 577-3300

Mayor's Office ☎ 788-7585

Mayor's Office for People With Disabilities ☎ 788-2830

Medicaid ☎ 718/291-1900

Medicare ☎ 800/638-6833

NY Post Office ☎ 967-8585

NY Public Library Telephone Reference Service ☎ 340-0849

Overeaters Anonymous ☎ 206-8621

Passport Information ☎ 206-3500

Planned Parenthood ☎ 274-7200

Social Security ☎ 800/772-1213

Taxi Complaints ☎ 302-8294

Time ☎ 976-2928

Towaways ☎ 869-2929

Traffic Information ☎ 787-3387

Traveler's Aid ☎ 944-0013

24-Hour Locksmith ☎ 247-6747

UN Information ☎ 963-1234

US Customs ☎ 800/697-3662

Weather ☎ 970-1212

TOURS

Adventure on a Shoestring ☎ 265-2663

Art Tours ☎ 239-4160

Big Onion Walking Tours ☎ 439-1090

Circle Line ☎ 563-3200

Doorways to Design ☎ 718/339-1542

Gray Line ☎ 397-2600

Harlem Renaissance ☎ 862-7200

Island Helicopter ☎ 564-9290

Liberty Helicopter ☎ 967-6464

NY Apple Tours ☎ 800/876-9868

NY Talks and Walks ☎ 888/377-4455

NYC Cultural Walking Tours ☎ 979-2388

NYC Discovery Tours ☎ 465-3331

The Petrel (1938) ☎ 825-1976

Seaport Liberty Cruises ☎ 630-8388

Spirit Cruises of NY ☎ 727-2789

World Yacht Cruises ☎ 630-8100

PARKS AND RECREATION

Acqueduct & Belmont Race Tracks
☎ 718/641-4700

Bryant Park ☎ 983-4142

Central Park Information
☎ 360-3444

Continental Arena ☎ 201/935-3900

Empire Skate Club ☎ 774-1774

Five Boro Bicycle Club ☎ 932-2300

Giants Stadium ☎ 201/935-8222

Jets Information ☎ 516/560-8200

Madison Square Garden
☎ 465-6741

Meadowlands Race Track
☎ 201/935-8500

Meadowlands Sports Complex
☎ 201/935-3900

Nassau Coliseum ☎ 516/794-9300

NY Knicks Hotline ☎ 465-5867

NY Islanders ☎ 516/794-4100

NY Mets ☎ 718/507-8499

NY Road Runners ☎ 860-2280

NY Yankees ☎ 718/293-6000

Parks Events ☎ 360-3456

Shea Stadium ☎ 718/507-8499

Sports Phone ☎ 976-1313

US Open Tennis ☎ 718/760-6200

Yonkers Raceway ☎ 914/968-4200

Zoo/Central Park ☎ 861-6030

Zoo/Bronx ☎ 718/220-5100

TRANSPORTATION

Access-a-Ride ☎ 632-7272

Adirondack Pine Hill/Trailways
☎ 800/225-6815

Airport Bus Service ☎ 718/706-9658

Amtrak ☎ 800/872-7245;
800/523-8720

Bonanza Bus Lines ☎ 800/556-3815

Bus & Subway Information
☎ 718/330-1234; 718/858-7272

Bus & Subway Accessibility
☎ 718/596-8585

Ellis Island/Statue of Liberty Ferry
☎ 269-5755

EZ Pass Information
☎ 800/333-8655

Gray Line Air Shuttle ☎ 977-9433

Greyhound Bus Lines
☎ 800/231-2222

Hoboken Ferry (NJ) ☎ 201/420-4422

JFK Airport ☎ 718/244-4444

La Guardia Airport ☎ 718/533-3400

Long Island Railroad (LIRR)
☎ 718/217-5477

Martz Trailways ☎ 800/233-8604

Metro North ☎ 532-4900

NJ Transit ☎ 800/626-7433;
973/762-5100

New York Waterway Ferries
☎ 800/53-FERRY

Newark Airport ☎ 973/961-6000

Olympia Express ☎ 964-6233

Passenger Ship Terminal
☎ 246-5451

PATH ☎ 800/234-7284

Peter Pan Bus Lines ☎ 413/781-2900

Port Authority Bus Information
☎ 564-8484; 564-1111

Port Authority Heliport ☎ 248-7240

Roosevelt Island Tram ☎ 832-4543

SeaStreak Ferry ☎ 800/262-8743

Short Line ☎ 736-4700

Staten Island Ferry ☎ 718/390-5253

**Triborough Bridge and Tunnel
Authority** ☎ 360-3000

Vermont Transit ☎ 802/862-9671

ENTERTAINMENT

Alliance of Resident Theatres
☎ 989-5257

Big Apple Circus ☎ 268-2500

Broadway Line ☎ 320-4111

Carnegie Hall ☎ 247-7800

City Center ☎ 581-1212

Comedy Clubline ☎ 718/4-COMEDY

Jazz Line ☎ 479-7888

Lincoln Center ☎ 546-2656

Movie Phone ☎ 777-FILM

NYC On Stage ☎ 768-1818

Radio City Music Hall ☎ 247-4777

**Reduced Price Theatre Tickets
(TKTS)** ☎ 768-1818

Restaurant Phone ☎ 777-FOOD

Telecharge ☎ 239-6200

Ticket Central ☎ 279-4200

Ticketmaster ☎ 307-7171

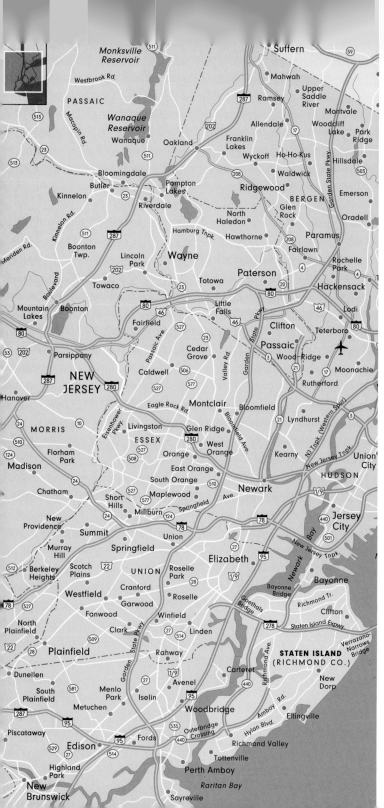

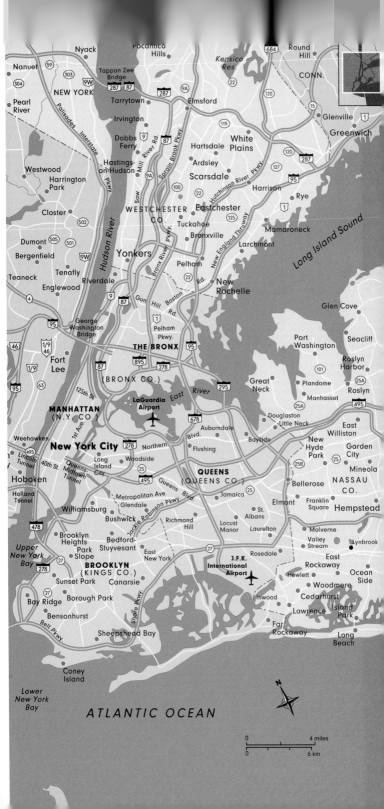

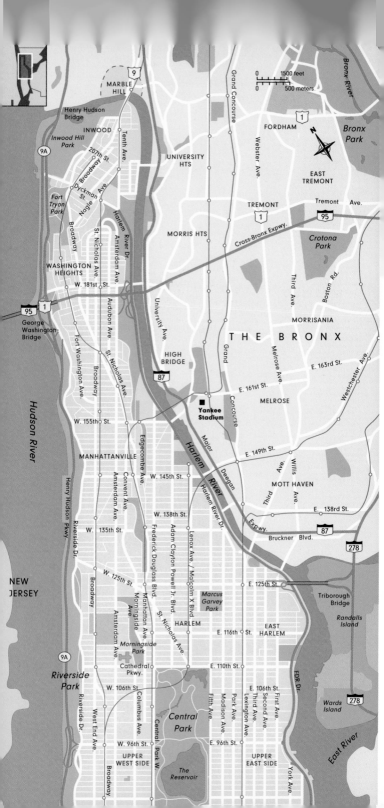

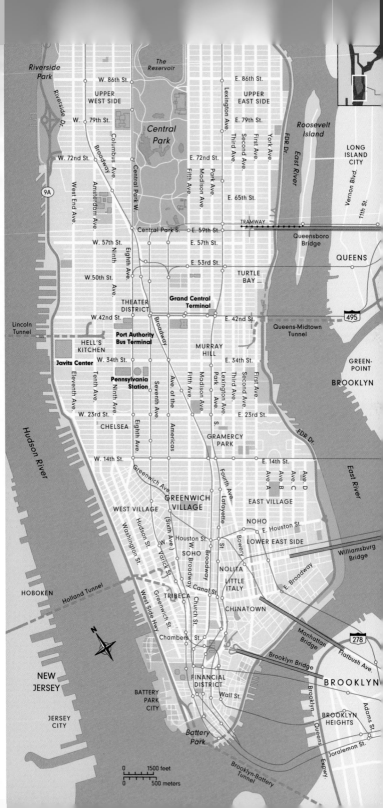

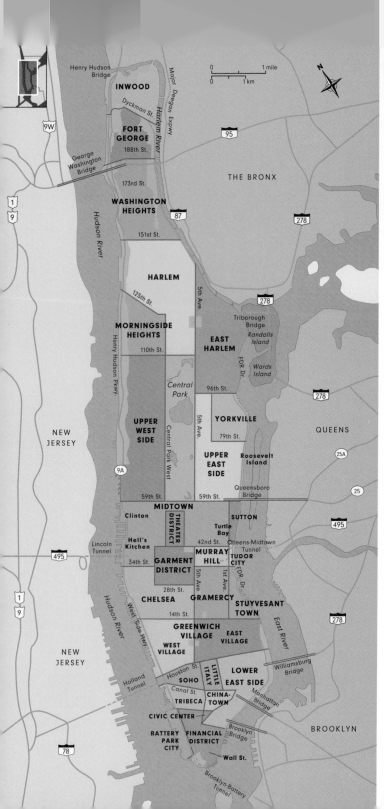

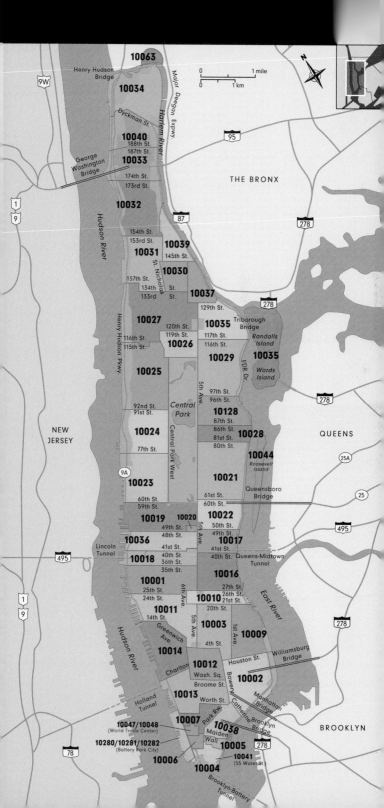

Streets	West End Ave.	Broadway	Amsterdam Ave.	Columbus Ave.	Central Park West
94–96	700–737	2520–2554	702–733	701–740	350–360
92–94	660–699	2476–2519	656–701	661–700	322–336
90–92	620–659	2440–2475	620–655	621–660	300–320
88–90	578–619	2401–2439	580–619	581–620	279–295
86–88	540–577	2361–2400	540–579	541–580	262–275
84–86	500–539	2321–2360	500–539	501–540	241–257
82–84	460–499	2281–2320	460–499	461–500	212–239
80–82	420–459	2241–2280	420–459	421–460	211
78–80	380–419	2201–2240	380–419	381–420	American Museum of Natural History
76–78	340–379	2161–2200	340–379	341–380	
74–76	300–339	2121–2160	300–339	301–340	145–160
72–74	262–299	2081–2114	261–299	261–300	121–135
70–72	221–261	2040–2079	221–260	221–260	101–115
68–70	176–220	1999–2030	181–220	181–220	80–99
66–68	122–175	1961–1998	140–180	141–180	65–79
64–66	74–121	1920–1960	100–139	101–140	50–55
62–64	44–73	Lincoln Center	60–99	61–100	25–33
60–62	20–43	1841–1880	20–59	21–60	15
58–60	2–19	Columbus Circle	1–19	2–20	Columbus Circle

	11th Ave.	Broadway	10th Ave.	9th Ave.	8th Ave.	7th Ave.	6th Ave.
56–58	823–854	1752–1791	852–889	864–907	946–992	888–921	1381–1419
54–56	775–822	1710–1751	812–851	824–863	908–945	842–887	1341–1377
52–54	741–774	1674–1709	772–811	782–823	870–907	798–841	1301–1330
50–52	701–740	1634–1673	737–770	742–781	830–869	761–797	1261–1297
48–50	665–700	1596–1633	686–735	702–741	791–829	720–760	1221–1260
46–48	625–664	1551–1595	654–685	662–701	735–790	701–719	1180–1217
44–46	589–624	1514–1550	614–653	622–661	701–734	Times Square	1141–1178
42–44	553–588	1472–1513	576–613	582–621	661–700		1100–1140
40–42	503–552	1440–1471	538–575	Port Authority	620–660	560–598	1061–1097
38–40	480–502	1400–1439	502–537		570–619	522–559	1020–1060
36–38	431–471	1352–1399	466–501	468–501	520–569	482–521	981–1019
34–36	405–430	Macy's	430–465	432–467	480–519	442–481	Herald Square
32–34	360–404	1260–1282	380–429	412–431	442–479	Penn Station	
30–32	319–359	1220–1279	341–379	Post Office	403–441	362–399	855–892
28–30	282–318	1178–1219	314–340	314–351	362–402	322–361	815–844
26–28	242–281	1135–1177	288–313	262–313	321–361	282–321	775–814
24–26	202–241	1100–1134	239–287	230–261	281–320	244–281	733–774
22–24	162–201	940–1099	210–238	198–229	236–280	210–243	696–732
20–22	120–161	902–939	162–209	167–197	198–235	170–209	656–695
18–20	82–119	873–901	130–161	128–166	162–197	134–169	613–655
16–18	54–81	860–872	92–129	92–127	126–161	100–133	574–612
14–16	26–53	Union Square	58–91	91–44	80–125	64–99	573–530

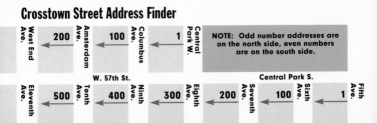

Crosstown Street Address Finder

West End Ave. ← 200 ← Amsterdam Ave. ← 100 ← Columbus Ave. ← 1 ← Central Park W.

NOTE: Odd number addresses are on the north side, even numbers are on the south side.

W. 57th St.

Central Park S.

Eleventh Ave. ← 500 ← Tenth Ave. ← 400 ← Ninth Ave. ← 300 ← Eighth Ave. ← 200 ← Seventh Ave. ← 100 ← Sixth Ave. ← 1 ← Fifth Ave.

5th Ave.	Madison Ave.	Park Ave.	Lexington Ave.	3rd Ave.	2nd Ave.	1st Ave.	Streets
1130–1148	1340–1379	1199–1236	1449–1486	1678–1709	1817–1868	1817–1855	**94–96**
1109–1125	1295–1335	1160–1192	1400–1444	1644–1677	1766–1808	1780–1811	**92–94**
1090–1107	1254–1294	1120–1155	1361–1396	1601–1643	1736–1763	1740–1779	**90–92**
1070–1089	1220–1250	1080–1114	1311–1355	1568–1602	1700–1739	1701–1735	**88–90**
1050–1069	1178–1221	1044–1076	1280–1301	1530–1566	1660–1698	1652–1689	**86–88**
1030–1048	1130–1171	1000–1035	1248–1278	1490–1529	1624–1659	1618–1651	**84–86**
1010–1028	1090–1128	960–993	1210–1248	1450–1489	1584–1623	1578–1617	**82–84**
990–1009	1058–1088	916–959	1164–1209	1410–1449	1538–1583	1540–1577	**80–82**
970–989	1012–1046	878–911	1120–1161	1374–1409	1498–1537	1495–1539	**78–80**
950–969	974–1006	840–877	1080–1116	1330–1373	1456–1497	1462–1494	**76–78**
930–947	940–970	799–830	1036–1071	1290–1329	1420–1454	1429–1460	**74–76**
910–929	896–939	760–791	1004–1032	1250–1289	1389–1417	1344–1384	**72–74**
895–907	856–872	720–755	962–993	1210–1249	1328–1363	1306–1343	**70–72**
870–885	813–850	680–715	926–961	1166–1208	1296–1327	1266–1300	**68–70**
850–860	772–811	640–679	900–922	1130–1165	1260–1295	1222–1260	**66–68**
830–849	733–771	600–639	841–886	1084–1129	1222–1259	1168–1221	**64–66**
810–828	690–727	560–599	803–842	1050–1083	1180–1221	1130–1167	**62–64**
790–807	654–680	520–559	770–802	1010–1049	1140–1197	1102–1129	**60–62**
755–789	621–649	476–519	722–759	972–1009	Queensborough Bridge		**58–60**
720–754	572–611	434–475	677–721	942–968	1066–1101	1026–1063	**56–58**
680–719	532–568	408–430	636–665	894–933	1028–1062	985–1021	**54–56**
656–679	500–531	360–399	596–629	856–893	984–1027	945–984	**52–54**
626–655	452–488	320–350	556–593	818–855	944–983	889–944	**50–52**
600–625	412–444	280–300	518–555	776–817	902–943	860–888	**48–50**
562–599	377–400	240–277	476–515	741–775	862–891	827	**46–48**
530–561	346–375	**Met Life** (200)	441–475	702–735	824–860	785 _United Nations_	**44–46**
500–529	316–345	**Grand Central**	395–435	660–701	793–823		**42–44**
460–499	284–315		354–394	622–659	746–773	**Tudor City**	**40–42**
424–459	250–283	68–99	314–353	578–621	707–747	666–701	**38–40**
392–423	218–249	40–67 _Park Ave._	284–311	542–577	666–700	**Midtown Tunnel**	**36–38**
352–391	188–217	5–35	240–283	508–541	622–659	599–626	**34–36**
320–351	152–184	1–4	196–239	470–507	585–621	556–598	**32–34**
284–319	118–150	444–470 _Park Ave. S._	160–195	432–469	543–581	**Kips Bay**	**30–32**
250–283	79–117	404–431	120–159 _Lexington Ave._	394–431	500–541	**NYU Hosp.**	**28–30**
213–249	50–78	364–403	81–119	358–393	462–499	446–478	**26–28**
201–212	11–37	323–361	40–77	321–355	422–461	411–445	**24–26**
172–200	1–7	286–322	9–39	282–318	382–421	390–410	**22–24**
154–170		251–285	1–8 _Irving Pl._	244–281	344–381	315–389	**20–22**
109–153		221–250	70–78	206–243	310–343	310–314	**18–20**
85–127		184–220	40–69	166–205	301–309	280–309	**16–18**
69–108		**Union Square**	2–30	126–165	230–240	240–279	**14–16**

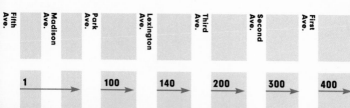

Fifth Ave.	Madison Ave.	Park Ave.	Lexington Ave.	Third Ave.	Second Ave.	First Ave.	
1 →		**100** →	**140** →	**200** →	**300** →	**400** →	

MAP 8 Streetfinder/The Village & Downtown

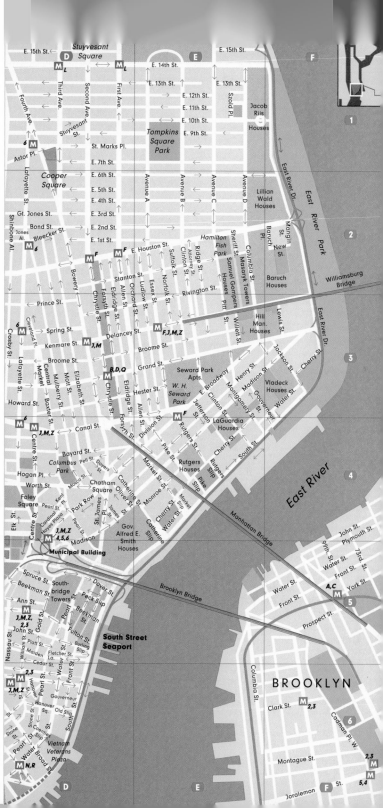

MAP 8 Streetfinder/The Village & Downtown

Letter codes refer to grid sectors on preceding map

Abingdon Sq. B1
Albany St. B6, C5
Allen St. D2, D3
Ann St. C5, D5
Astor Pl. D1
Attorney St. E2
Ave. A E1, E2
Ave. B E1, E2
Ave. C E1, E2
Ave. D E1, E2
Ave. of the Americas (Sixth Ave.) C1, C4
Bank St. A2, B1
Barclay St. C5
Barrow St. B2
Baruch Pl. F2
Battery Pl. C6
Baxter St. D3, D4
Bayard St. D4
Beach St. B4
Beaver St. C6, D6
Bedford St. B2, C2
Beekman St. D5
Bethune St. A1, B1
Bleecker St. B1, D2
Bond St. D2
Bowery D2, D4
Bowling Green C6
Bridge St. C6, D6
Broadway C1, C6
Brooklyn Battery Tunnel C6, D6
Brooklyn Bridge D5, F5
Broome St. B3, E3
Burling Slip D5
Canal St. C3, E3
Cardinal Hayes Plaza D4
Carlisle St. C6
Carmine St. B2
Catherine La. C4
Catherine Slip E4
Catherine St. D4, E4
Cedar St. C5, D5
Central Market D3
Centre St. D3, D5
Chambers St. B4, D4
Charles St. B1, B2

Charlton St. B3, C3
Chatham Sq. D4
Cherry St. E4, F3
Christopher St. B2, C1
Chrystie St. D2, D3
Church St. C4, C5
Clarkson St. B2, B3
Cleveland Pl. D3
Clinton St. E2, E4
Coenties Slip D6
Columbia St. E2, E3
Commerce St. B2
Cooper Sq. D1, D2
Cornelia St. B2
Cortlandt St. C5
Crosby St. C2, C3
Delancey St. D3, E3
Depyster St. D6
Desbrosses St. B3
Dey St. C5
Division St. D4, E4
Dominick St. B3, C3
Dover St. D5
Downing St. B2, C2
Doyers St. D4
Duane St. C4, D4
East Broadway D4, E3
East Houston St. D2, F2
East River Drive F1, F3
East Washington Pl. C2
Eighth Ave. B1
Eldridge St. D2, D3
Elizabeth St. D2, D4
Elk St. D4
Ericsson Pl. C4
Essex St. E2, E3
Exchange Pl. C6, D6
FDR Dr. F1, F3
Father Demo Sq. C2
Federal Plaza C4, D4
Fifth Ave. C1
First Ave. D1, D2
Fletcher St. D5
Foley Sq. D4
Forsyth St. D4, E4
Fourth Ave. D1
Franklin St. C4

Front St. D6
Fulton St. C5, D5
Gansevoort St. A1, B1
Gay St. B1, C1
Gold St. D5
Gouverneur La. D6
Gouverneur St. E3
Grand St. C3, F3
Great Jones St. D2
Greene St. C1, C3
Greenwich Ave. B1, C1
Greenwich St. B1, C6
Grove St. B2
Hanover Sq. D6
Hanover St. D6
Harrison St. B4, C4
Henry St. D4, E3
Hester St. D3, E3
Hogan Pl. D4
Holland Tunnel A4, C3
Horatio St. A1, B1
Hubert St. B4
Hudson St. B1, C4
Independence Plaza B4, C4
Jackson St. F3
James St. D4
Jane St. A1, B1
Jay St. C4
Jefferson St. E3
John St. C5, D5
Jones Alley D2
Jones St. B2
Kenmare St. D3
Kent Pl. D4
King St. B3, C3
Lafayette St. D1, D4
LaGuardia Pl. C2
Laight St. B4
Leonard St. C4
Leroy St. B2
Lewis St. F3
Liberty St. C5
Lispenard St. C4
Little W. 12th St. A1
Ludlow St. E2, E3
MacDougal Alley C1
MacDougal St. C1, C3

MAP 9 Hospitals & Late-Night Pharmacies

Listed Alphabetically

HOSPITALS

Bellevue Hospital Center, 28.
462 First Ave ☎ 562-4141

Beth Israel Med Center, 32.
First Ave at 16th St ☎ 420-2000

Beth Israel North, 9.
170 East End Ave ☎ 870-9000

Cabrini Med Center, 30. 227 E 19th St
☎ 995-6000

Coler Memorial, 10. 900 Main St,
Roosevelt Island ☎ 848-6000

Columbia–Presbyterian Med Ctr, 1.
622 W 168th St ☎ 305-2500

Goldwater Memorial, 24. 1 Main St,
Roosevelt Island ☎ 318-8000

Gouverneur, 39. 227 Madison St
☎ 238-7000

Gracie Square (Psychiatric), 14.
420 E 76th St ☎ 988-4400

Harlem Hospital Center, 2.
506 Lenox Ave ☎ 939-1000

Joint Diseases, 31. 301 E 17th St
☎ 598-6000

Lenox Hill, 12. 100 E 77th St
☎ 434-2000

Manhattan Eye, Ear, & Throat, 19.
210 E 64th St ☎ 838-9200

**Memorial Sloan-Kettering (Cancer),
18.** 1275 York Ave ☎ 639-2000

Metropolitan, 6. 1901 First Ave
☎ 423-6262

Mount Sinai, 5. Fifth Ave at 100th St
☎ 241-6500

New York Cornell Med Center, 16.
525 E 68th St ☎ 746-5454

New York Downtown, 40.
170 William St ☎ 312-5000

New York Eye & Ear, 33. 310 E 14th St
☎ 979-4000

NYU Med Center, 27. 550 First Ave
☎ 263-7300

Payne Whitney (Psychiatric), 14.
420 E 76th St ☎ 746-3800

St Luke's–Roosevelt, 20.
1000 Tenth Ave ☎ 523-4000

Special Surgery, 15. 535 E 70th St
☎ 606-1000

St Clare's, 22. 415 W 51st St
☎ 586-1500

St Luke's–Roosevelt, 4. 1111
Amsterdam Ave ☎ 523-4000

St Vincent's, 34. 153 W 11th St
☎ 604-7000

VA Hospital, 29. 408 First Ave
☎ 686-7500

LATE-NIGHT PHARMACIES

Bigelow Pharmacy, 35. 414 Sixth Ave
☎ 533-2700

Chung Wah Pharmacy, 38.
65 Mott St ☎ 587-4160

CVS Pharmacy, 26. 272 Eighth Ave
☎ 255-2592

Duane Reade, 7. 2465 Broadway
☎ 799-3172

Duane Reade, 13. 1279 Third Ave
☎ 744-2668

Duane Reade, 21. 224 W. 57th St
☎ 541-9708

Duane Reade, 37. 378 Sixth Ave
☎ 674-5357

Genovese, 17. 1299 Second Ave
☎ 772-0104

Irmat Pharmacy, 8. 531 Columbus
Ave ☎ 362-2350

Metropolis Drug Co, 25. 721 Ninth
Ave ☎ 246-0168

Pollock-Bailey Pharmacy, 23.
405 E 57th St ☎ 355-6094

Star Pharmacy, 11. 1540 First Ave
☎ 737-4324

Village Apothecary, 36.
346 Bleecker St ☎ 807-7566

Listed Alphabetically

American Academy of Dramatic Arts, 30. 120 Madison Ave
☎ 686-9244

Art Students' League, 24.
215 W 57th St ☎ 247-4510

Bank St College, 10. 610 W 112th St
☎ 875-4400

Bard Graduate Center, 12.
18 W 86th St ☎ 501-3000

Barnard College, 7. 3009 Broadway
☎ 854-5262

Baruch College, 32. 17 Lexington Ave
☎ 802-2000

Borough of Manhattan Community College, 48. 199 Chambers Street
☎ 346-8000

Cardozo Law, 34. 55 Fifth Ave
☎ 790-0200

Circle in the Square, 26.
1633 Broadway ☎ 307-0388

City College of NY, 3.
Convent Ave & 138th St ☎ 650-7000

Columbia Physicians & Surgeons, 2.
630 W 168th St ☎ 305-2500

Columbia University, 8.
B'way & 116th St ☎ 854-1754

Cooper Union, 37.
30 Cooper Sq ☎ 353-4100

Cornell Medical Center, 18.
1300 York Ave ☎ 746-5454

CUNY Graduate School and University Center, 27. 265 Fifth Ave
☎ 817-7000

Fashion Institute of Technology, 31.
227 W 27th St ☎ 217-7675

Fordham University School of Law, 23.
140 W 62nd St ☎ 636-6810

Fordham University, 22.
113 W 60th St ☎ 636-6000

The French Culinary Institute, 45.
462 Broadway ☎ 219-8890

Hebrew Union, 39. 1 W 4th St
☎ 674-5300

Hunter College, 17. 695 Park Ave
☎ 772-4000

Jewish Theological Seminary, 5.
Broadway & 122nd St ☎ 678-8000

John Jay College, 25.
445 W 59th St ☎ 237-8000

Juilliard School of Music, 20.
60 Lincoln Center Pl ☎ 799-5000

Leonard N. Stern School of Business at NYU, 38. 44 W 4th
St ☎ 998-0600

Manhattan School of Music, 4.
120 Claremont Ave ☎ 749-2802

Mannes College of Music, 13.
150 W 85th St ☎ 580-0210

Martha Graham School, 42.
440 Lafayette St ☎ 838-5886

Marymount College, 14. 221 E 71st St
☎ 517-0400

Mount Sinai School of Medicine, 11.
Fifth Ave & 100th St ☎ 241-6696

New School, 36. 66 W 12th St
☎ 229-5600

NY Institute of Technology, 16.
1855 Broadway ☎ 261-1500

NY Law School, 47. 47 Worth St
☎ 431-2100

NY Restaurant School, 46.
75 Varick St ☎ 226-5500

NY School of Interior Design, 15.
170 E 70th St ☎ 472-1500

NYU, 41. Washington Sq ☎ 998-1212

NYU Law School, 40. 110 W 3rd St
☎ 998-6060

NYU Medical Center, 28.
550 First Ave ☎ 263-5290

Pace University, 49. 1 Pace Plaza
☎ 346-1200

Parsons School of Design, 35.
66 Fifth Ave ☎ 229-8900

Pratt Manhattan, 44.
295 Lafayette St ☎ 925-8481

Rockefeller University, 19.
York Ave & 66th St ☎ 327-8000

School of American Ballet, 21.
70 Lincoln Center Pl ☎ 877-0600

School of Visual Arts, 33.
209 E 23rd St ☎ 592-2000

Stella Adler Conservatory, 43.
419 Lafayette St ☎ 260-0525

SUNY College of Optometry, 30.
100 E 24th St ☎ 780-4900

Teachers College, 9. 525 W 120th St
☎ 678-3000

Union Theological Seminary, 6.
Broadway & 120th St ☎ 662-7100

Yeshiva University, 1.
Amsterdam Ave & 185th St
☎ 960-5400

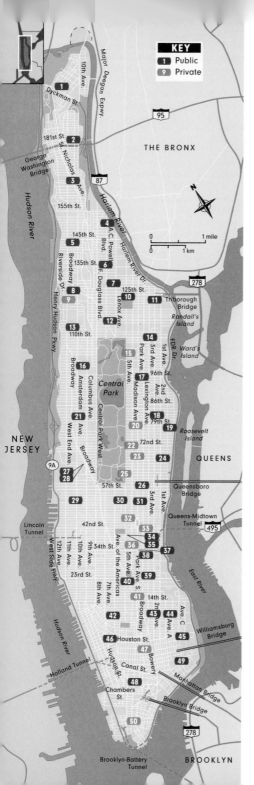

KEY

1 Public
9 Private

THE BRONX

NEW JERSEY

QUEENS

BROOKLYN

Listed by Site Number

Listed Alphabetically

CONSULATES

Afghanistan, 79. 360 Lexington Ave ☎ 972-2277

Argentina, 23. 12 W 56th St ☎ 603-0400

Australia, 80. 150 E 42nd St ☎ 351-6500

Austria, 11. 31 E 69th St ☎ 737-6400

Bahamas, 54. 231 E 46th St ☎ 421-6420

Bahrain, 62. 2 UN Plaza ☎ 223-6200

Bangladesh, 68. 211 E 43rd St ☎ 599-6767

Barbados, 69. 800 Second Ave ☎ 867-8431

Belgium, 30. 1330 Sixth Ave ☎ 586-5110

Bhutan, 62. 2 UN Plaza ☎ 826-1919

Bolivia, 68. 211 E 43rd St ☎ 687-0530

Brazil, 99. 421 Seventh Ave ☎ 916-3201

Canada, 29. 1251 Sixth Ave ☎ 596-1700

Chile, 48. 866 UN Plaza ☎ 980-3366

China, 75. 520 Twelfth Ave ☎ 330-7400

Colombia, 59. 10 E 46th St ☎ 949-9898

Costa Rica, 98. 80 Wall St ☎ 425-2620

Cyprus, 78. 13 E 40th St ☎ 686-6016

Denmark, 49. 885 Second Ave ☎ 223-4545

Dominican Republic, 74. 1501 Broadway ☎ 768-2480

Ecuador, 69. 800 Second Ave ☎ 808-0170

Egypt, 20. 1110 Second Ave ☎ 759-7120

El Salvador, 92. 46 Park Ave ☎ 889-3608

Estonia, 85. 600 Third Ave ☎ 883-0636

Fiji, 63. 630 Third Ave ☎ 687-4130

Finland, 48. 866 UN Plaza ☎ 750-4400

France, 7. 934 Fifth Ave ☎ 606-3688

Germany, 40. 871 UN Pl ☎ 610-9700

Ghana, 56. 19 E 47th St ☎ 832-1300

Great Britain, 34. 845 Third Ave ☎ 745-0202

Greece, 2. 69 E 79th St ☎ 988-5500

Grenada, 69. 800 Second Ave ☎ 599-0301

Guatemala, 94. 57 Park Ave ☎ 686-3837

Guyana, 48. 866 UN Plaza ☎ 527-3215

Haiti, 75. 271 Madison Ave ☎ 697-9767

Honduras, 98. 80 Wall St ☎ 269-3611

Hungary, 25. 223 E 52nd St ☎ 752-0661

Iceland, 41. 800 Third Ave ☎ 593-2700

India, 18. 3 E 64th St ☎ 774-0600

Indonesia, 12. 5 E 68th St ☎ 879-0600

Ireland, 32. 345 Park Ave ☎ 319-2555

Israel, 69. 800 Second Ave ☎ 499-5000

Italy, 10. 690 Park Ave ☎ 737-9100

Jamaica, 55. 767 Third Ave ☎ 935-9000

Japan, 47. 299 Park Ave ☎ 371-8222

Kenya, 46. 424 Madison Ave ☎ 486-1300

Korea, 22. 460 Park Ave ☎ 752-1700

Lebanon, 6. 9 E 76th St ☎ 744-7905

Liberia, 66. 820 Second Ave ☎ 687-1033

Lithuania, 97. 420 Fifth Ave ☎ 354-7840

Luxembourg, 39. 17 Beekman Pl ☎ 888-6664

Malaysia, 67. 313 E 43rd St ☎ 490-2722

Mexico, 96. 27 E 39th St ☎ 217-6400

Monaco, 57. 565 Fifth Ave ☎ 286-3330

Morocco, 76. 10 E 40th St ☎ 758-2625

Nepal, 66. 820 Second Ave ☎ 370-3988

Netherlands, 45. 1 Rockefeller Plaza ☎ 246-1429

New Zealand, 43. 780 Third Ave ☎ 832-4038

Nigeria, 65. 828 Second Ave ☎ 808-0301

Norway, 37. 825 Third Ave ☎ 421-7333

Pakistan, 17. 12 E 65th St ☎ 879-5800

Paraguay, 73. 675 Third Ave ☎ 682-9441

Peru, 42. 215 Lexington Ave ☎ 481-7410

Poland, 95. 233 Madison Ave ☎ 889-8360

Portugal, 31. 630 Fifth Ave ☎ 765-2980

Airlines

Terminals

Airlines	JFK	LA GUARDIA	NEWARK
Aer Lingus ☎ 888/474-7424	4E		B
Aeroflot ☎ 212/332-1050	3		
Aerolineas Argentinas ☎ 800/333-0276	8		
AeroMexico ☎ 800/237-6639	2		B
Air Afrique ☎ 800/237-2747	4W		
Air Aruba ☎ 800/882-7822			B
Air Canada ☎ 800/776-3000		CTB-A	A
Air China ☎ 212/371-9898		Delta	
Air France ☎ 800/237-2747	1		B
Air India ☎ 212/751-6200	4W		
Air Jamaica ☎ 800/523-5585	2,3		B
Air Nova ☎ 800/776-3000		CTB-A	A
Air Ontario ☎ 800/776-3000		CTB-A	A
Alitalia ☎ 800/223-5730	4E		B,C
ALIA-Royal Jordanian ☎ 212/949-0050	5		
All Nippon Airways ☎ 800/235-9262	3		
American ☎ 800/433-7300	8, 9	CTB-D	A,B
American Eagle ☎ 800/433-7300	9		
American Trans Air ☎ 800/435-9282	4E	CTB-C	
America West ☎ 800/235-9292	6	CTB-A	C
Asiana Airlines ☎ 800/227-4262	8		
Austrian Airlines ☎ 800/843-0002	3		
Avianca ☎ 800/284-2622	3		B
Biman Bangladesh ☎ 212/808-4477	4E		
British Airways ☎ 800/247-9297	7		B
Business Express ☎ 800/345-3400	3	Delta	
BWIA ☎ 800/538-2942	4E		
Canadian Airlines ☎ 800/426-7000	9	CTB-D	
Carnival ☎ 800/437-2110	4E	CTB-C	B
Cathay Pacific ☎ 800/233-2742	3		
China Airlines ☎ 800/227-5118	3		
Colgan Air ☎ 800/272-5488		CTB-B	C

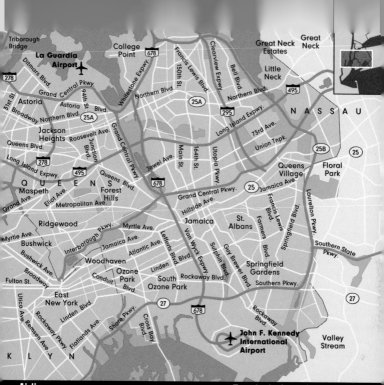

Airlines

	JFK	LA GUARDIA	NEWARK
		Terminals (cont.)	
Continental ☎ 800/525-0280		CTB-A	A,B,C
Continental Express ☎ 800/525-0280		CTB-A	C
Czech Airlines ☎ 212/765-6022			B
Delta ☎ 800/221-1212	3	Delta	B
Delta Shuttle ☎ 800/221-1212		MAT	
Egypt Air ☎ 212/315-0900	4E		
El-Al ☎ 800/223-6700	4W		B
EVA Airways ☎ 800/695-1188			B
Finnair ☎ 800/950-5000	2		
Ghana Airways ☎ 800/404-4262	4E		
Guyana ☎ 718/693-8000	4E		
Iberia ☎ 800/772-4642	9		
Icelandair ☎ 800/223-5500	7		
Japan ☎ 800/525-3663	1		
KIWI ☎ 800/538-5494	4E		A
KLM ☎ 212/759-3600; 800/374-7747	4E		
Korean ☎ 800/438-5000	1		B
Kuwait ☎ 212/308-5454	4E		
Lacsa Airlines ☎ 800/225-2272	3		
Lan Chile ☎ 800/488-0070	7		
LOT Polish ☎ 800/223-0593	8		B
Lufthansa ☎ 800/645-3880	1		B
Malev Hungarian ☎ 212/757-6446	3		
Mexicana ☎ 800/531-7921			B
Midway ☎ 800/446-4392		CTB-D	A
Midwest Express ☎ 800/452-2022		CTB-C	B
North American ☎ 718/656-2650	4E		B
Northwest ☎ 800/225-2525	4E	Delta	B

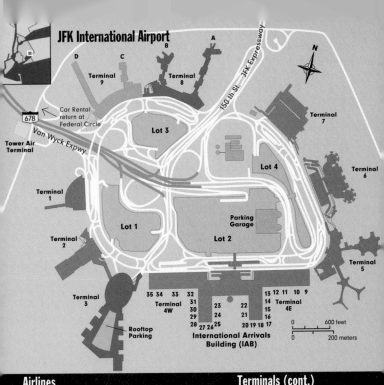

JFK International Airport

678

Van Wyck Expwy.

Car Rental return at Federal Circle

Tower Air Terminal

Terminal 9
Terminal 8
Terminal 7
Terminal 6
Terminal 5
Terminal 1
Terminal 2
Terminal 3

150 th St.
JFK Expressway

N

Lot 3
Lot 4
Lot 1
Lot 2

Parking Garage

Rooftop Parking

Terminal 4W
35 34 33 32
31
30
29
28 27 26 25

23
24

22

International Arrivals Building (IAB)

13 12 11 10 9
14
15
16
20 19 18 17

Terminal 4E

0   600 feet
0   200 meters

Airlines

	JFK	LA GUARDIA	NEWARK
Olympic ☏ 212/838-3600	1		
Pakistan ☏ 212/370-9158	4W		
Qantas ☏ 800/227-4500	9		A
Royal Air Maroc ☏ 212/750-6071	1		
SAS ☏ 800/221-2350			B
Sabena ☏ 800/955-2000	3		B
Singapore Airlines ☏ 800/742-3333	1		B
South African Airways ☏ 800/722-9675	8		
Sun Country ☏ 800/359-5786	5		
Swissair ☏ 800/221-4750	3		B
Tarom-Romanian ☏ 212/687-6013	4E		
TACA International ☏ 800/535-8780	2		
TAP Air Portugal ☏ 800/221-7370	3		B
Tower Air ☏ 718/553-8500	Tower		
TransBrasil ☏ 800/872-3153		Delta	
Turkish Airlines ☏ 212/339-9650	1		
TW Express ☏ 800/221-2000	5		
TWA ☏ 800/221-2000	5	Main	A
United ☏ 800/241-6522	7	CTB-C	A
United Express ☏ 800/241-6522	7	CTB-C	A
US Airways ☏ 800/428-4322		US Airways	A
US Airways Express ☏ 800/428-4322		US Airways	A
US Airways Shuttle ☏ 800/428-4322		US Airways Shuttle	
Uzbekistan Airways ☏ 212/489-3954	4E		
Varig ☏ 212/682-3100	4W		
VASP ☏ 800/732-8277	4W		C
Virgin Atlantic ☏ 800/862-8621	1		B

Terminals (cont.)

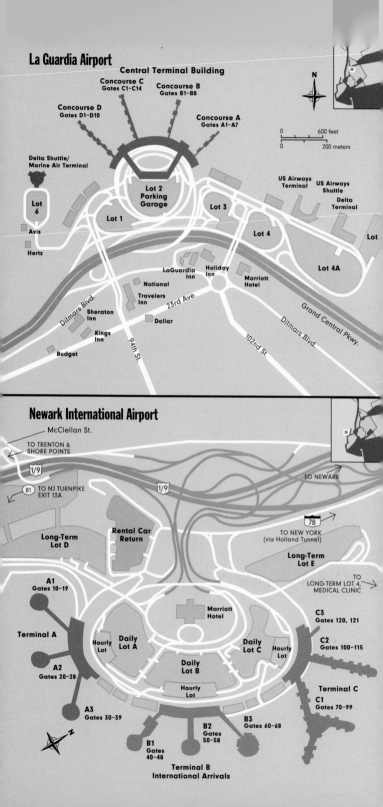

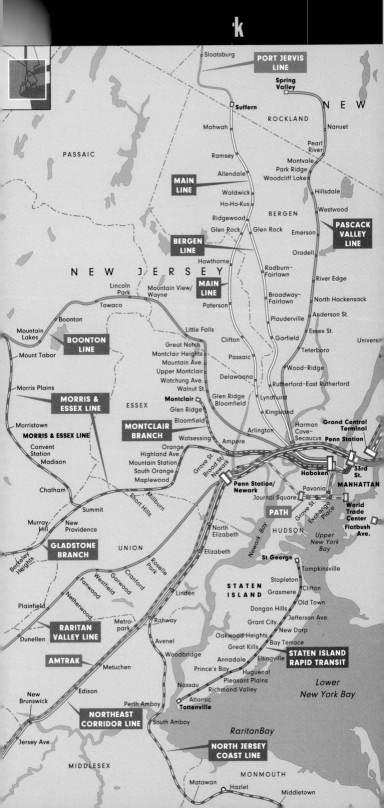

New Canaan
Springdale

Ossining
Chappaqua
Pleasantville
Scarborough

Y O R K
Hawthorne
Mount Pleasant
C O N N E C T I C U T

Philipse Manor
Valhalla
Glenbrook
Darien

AMTRAK
Norroton
Heights

HUDSON LINE
Stamford

Tarrytown
North White Plains
AMTRAK

Irvington
HARLEM LINE
Old Greenwich

Ardsley
White Plains
Cos Cob
Riverside

Dobbs Ferry
Hartsdale
Greenwich

Hastings
Scarsdale
Port Chester

W E S T C H E S T E R
Rye

Greystone
Crestwood
Harrison

Glenwood
Tuckahoe
Mamaroneck

Fleetwood
Bronxville
OYSTER BAY BRANCH

Mt. Vernon W.
Larchmont
Long Island Sound

Yonkers
Mount Vernon

Ludlow
Pelham
Locust Valley
Cold Spring Harbor

Riverdale
Wakefield
New Rochelle
Glen Cove

Spuyten Duyvil
Woodlawn
NEW HAVEN LINE
Glen Street
Oyster Bay

Marble Hill
Williams Bridge
Sea Cliff
PORT JEFFERSON BRANCH

sity Heights
Botanical Gardens
PORT WASHINGTON BRANCH
Glen Head

Morris Heights
Fordham
Greenvale
Syosset

Tremont
Port Washington
N A S S A U

B R O N X
AMTRAK
Roslyn

Melrose
Great Neck
Plandome
Albertson
Hicksville

129th St.
La Guardia Airport
East River
Manhasset Mineola
East Williston
Westbury
Bethpage

Huntspoint Ave.
Little Neck
New Hyde Park
Country Life Press
Carle Place

Woodside
Auburndale
Bayside
Merillon Ave.
Garden City
RONKONKOMA BRANCH

Broadway
Flushing Main St.
Douglaston
Nassau Blvd.
Stewart

Murray Hill
Shea Stadium
Forest Hills
Kew Gdns.
Floral Park
Bellerose
Hempstead
Massapequa

N
Q U E E N S
Jamaica
Queens Village
Hollis
St. Albans
Henpstead Gdns.
West Hempstead
Bellmore
Seaford
Wantagh

Nostrand Ave.
Locust Manor
Lakeview
Malverne
Westwood
Rockville Center
Merrick
Freeport

East New York
Laurelton
Rosedale
Valley Stream
Gibson
Lynbrook
Hewlett
Centre Ave
East Rockaway
Oceanside
Baldwin

B R O O K L Y N
Kennedy International Airport
Inwood
Lawrence
Woodmere
Cedarhurst
Island Park

Far Rockaway
Long Beach
BABYLON BRANCH/ MONTAUK BRANCH

A T L A N T I C   O C E A N

N

KEY	
	Amtrak
	Long Island Railroad
	Metro-North Commuter Railroad
	New Jersey Transit
	PATH (Port Authority Trans-Hudson)
	Staten Island Rapid Transit

0   10 miles
0   15 km

KEY

- **9** Subway line
- ◉ Terminal
- □ Express stop
- ○ Local stop
- ◉ Express and local stop
- ⬤ Free transfer (Local)
- ▣ Free transfer (Express)

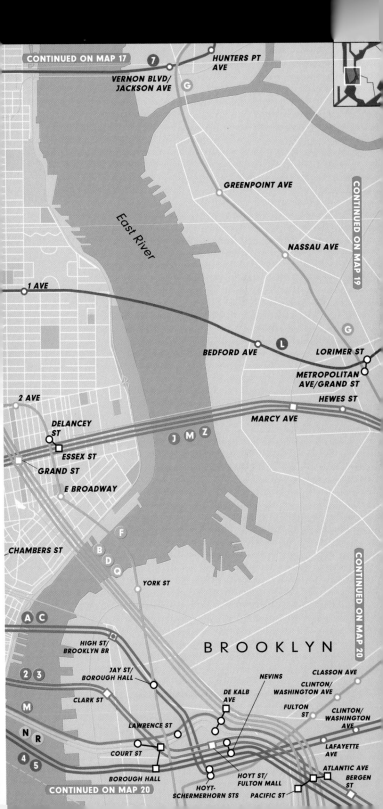

CONTINUED ON MAP 17

7 HUNTERS PT AVE

G VERNON BLVD/ JACKSON AVE

CONTINUED ON MAP 19

GREENPOINT AVE

East River

NASSAU AVE

1 AVE

G

BEDFORD AVE **L** LORIMER ST

METROPOLITAN AVE/GRAND ST

2 AVE

HEWES ST

DELANCEY ST

J M Z MARCY AVE

ESSEX ST

GRAND ST

E BROADWAY

F

CHAMBERS ST

B
D
Q YORK ST

A C

BROOKLYN

CONTINUED ON MAP 20

HIGH ST/ BROOKLYN BR

2 3 JAY ST/ BOROUGH HALL

CLASSON AVE

CLARK ST

NEVINS

CLINTON/ WASHINGTON AVE

DE KALB AVE

M

FULTON ST

CLINTON/ WASHINGTON AVE

LAWRENCE ST

N R

LAFAYETTE AVE

4 5 COURT ST

HOYT ST/ FULTON MALL

ATLANTIC AVE

BERGEN ST

BOROUGH HALL

HOYT- SCHERMERHORN STS

PACIFIC ST

CONTINUED ON MAP 20

MAP 17 | Subways/Manhattan 42nd St–125th St

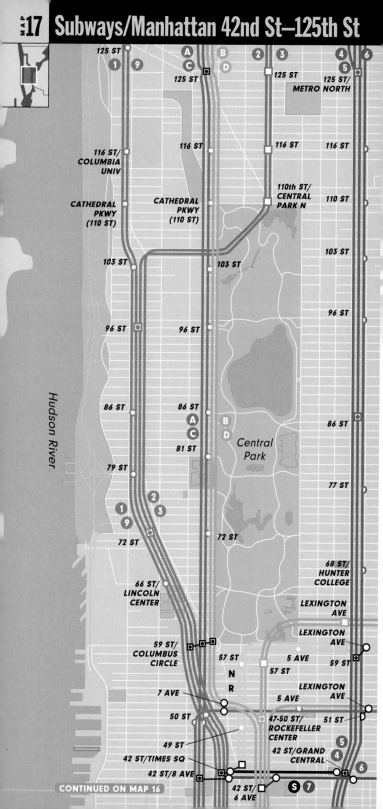

125 ST
1 **9**
Ⓐ **Ⓑ** **②** **③** **④** **⑥**
Ⓒ **Ⓓ** **⑤**
125 ST
125 ST
125 ST/ METRO NORTH

116 ST
116 ST
116 ST
116 ST
116 ST/ COLUMBIA UNIV

110th ST/ CENTRAL PARK N
110 ST
CATHEDRAL PKWY (110 ST)
CATHEDRAL PKWY (110 ST)

103 ST
103 ST
103 ST

96 ST
96 ST
96 ST

86 ST
86 ST
Ⓐ *Ⓑ*
Ⓒ *Ⓓ*
81 ST
86 ST

Central Park

79 ST
77 ST

1
②
③
9

72 ST
72 ST

68 ST/ HUNTER COLLEGE

66 ST/ LINCOLN CENTER

LEXINGTON AVE

LEXINGTON AVE

59 ST/ COLUMBUS CIRCLE
57 ST
5 AVE
59 ST
57 ST

N
R

LEXINGTON AVE
5 AVE

7 AVE
5 AVE

50 ST
51 ST

47-50 ST/ ROCKEFELLER CENTER

49 ST

42 ST/GRAND CENTRAL
⑤
④
42 ST/TIMES SQ
42 ST/8 AVE
⑥

CONTINUED ON MAP 16
42 ST/ 6 AVE
Ⓢ **⑦**

Hudson River

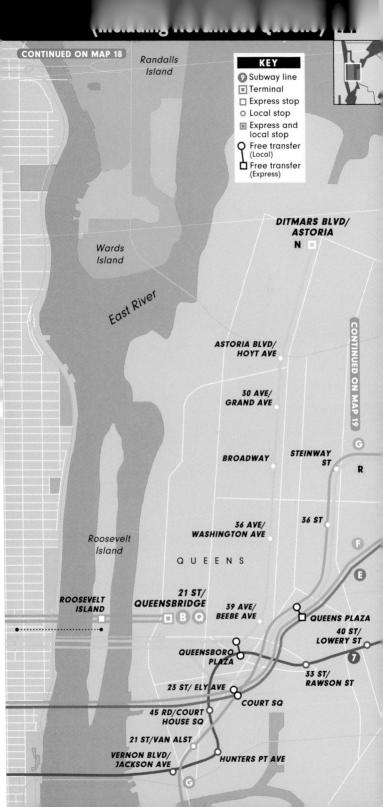

CONTINUED ON MAP 18

Randalls
Island

KEY

- **9** Subway line
- ▣ Terminal
- □ Express stop
- ○ Local stop
- ▣ Express and local stop
- Free transfer (Local)
- Free transfer (Express)

Wards
Island

East River

CONTINUED ON MAP 19

DITMARS BLVD/ ASTORIA
N ▣

ASTORIA BLVD/ HOYT AVE

30 AVE/ GRAND AVE

BROADWAY

STEINWAY ST

G

R

36 AVE/ WASHINGTON AVE

36 ST

Roosevelt
Island

QUEENS

F

E

ROOSEVELT ISLAND ▣

21 ST/ QUEENSBRIDGE ▣ **B** **Q**

39 AVE/ BEEBE AVE

QUEENS PLAZA ▣

40 ST/ LOWERY ST

QUEENSBORO PLAZA

33 ST/ RAWSON ST

7

23 ST/ ELY AVE

COURT SQ

45 RD/COURT HOUSE SQ

21 ST/VAN ALST

VERNON BLVD/ JACKSON AVE

HUNTERS PT AVE

G

MAP **18** Subways/Bronx & Northern Manhattan

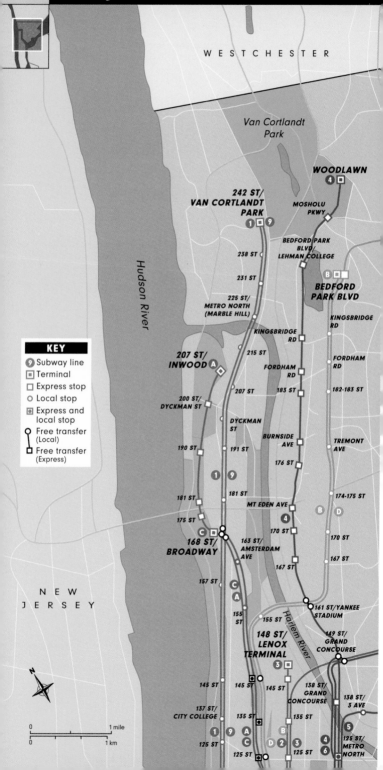

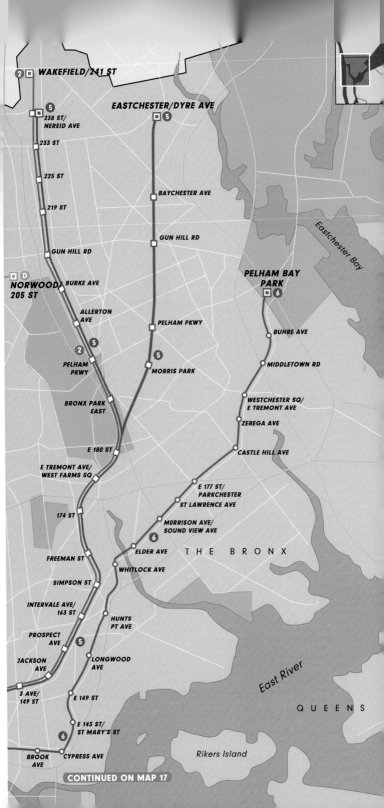

WAKEFIELD/241 ST
2

EASTCHESTER/DYRE AVE
5

238 ST/
NEREID AVE
5

233 ST

225 ST

219 ST

BAYCHESTER AVE

GUN HILL RD

GUN HILL RD

PELHAM BAY
PARK
6

NORWOOD
205 ST
D

BURKE AVE

ALLERTON
AVE

PELHAM PKWY

BUHRE AVE

MIDDLETOWN RD

2 5

PELHAM
PKWY

MORRIS PARK
5

Eastchester Bay

WESTCHESTER SQ/
E TREMONT AVE

BRONX PARK
EAST

ZEREGA AVE

E 180 ST

CASTLE HILL AVE

E TREMONT AVE/
WEST FARMS SQ

E 177 ST/
PARKCHESTER
ST LAWRENCE AVE

174 ST

MORRISON AVE/
SOUND VIEW AVE
6

FREEMAN ST

ELDER AVE

THE BRONX

WHITLOCK AVE

SIMPSON ST

INTERVALE AVE/
163 ST

HUNTS
PT AVE

PROSPECT
AVE

5

JACKSON
AVE

LONGWOOD
AVE

3 AVE/
149 ST

E 149 ST

East River

QUEENS

E 143 ST/
ST MARY'S ST
6

BROOK
AVE

CYPRESS AVE

Rikers Island

CONTINUED ON MAP 17

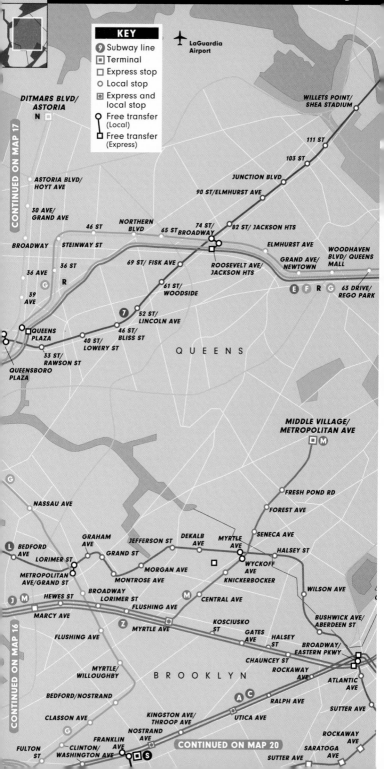

KEY

- **9** Subway line
- **▣** Terminal
- **□** Express stop
- **○** Local stop
- **▣** Express and local stop
- Free transfer (Local)
- Free transfer (Express)

✈ LaGuardia Airport

CONTINUED ON MAP 17

DITMARS BLVD/ ASTORIA
N

WILLETS POINT/ SHEA STADIUM

111 ST

103 ST

JUNCTION BLVD

90 ST/ELMHURST AVE

ASTORIA BLVD/ HOYT AVE

30 AVE/ GRAND AVE

46 ST

NORTHERN BLVD

65 ST

74 ST/ BROADWAY

82 ST/ JACKSON HTS

ELMHURST AVE

BROADWAY

STEINWAY ST

69 ST/ FISK AVE

ROOSEVELT AVE/ JACKSON HTS

GRAND AVE/ NEWTOWN

WOODHAVEN BLVD/ QUEENS MALL

36 AVE

36 ST

R

G

61 ST/ WOODSIDE

E F R G

63 DRIVE/ REGO PARK

39 AVE

7

52 ST/ LINCOLN AVE

QUEENS PLAZA

46 ST/ BLISS ST

40 ST/ LOWERY ST

QUEENS

33 ST/ RAWSON ST

QUEENSBORO PLAZA

MIDDLE VILLAGE/ METROPOLITAN AVE
M

G

NASSAU AVE

FRESH POND RD

FOREST AVE

SENECA AVE

GRAHAM AVE

JEFFERSON ST

DEKALB AVE

MYRTLE AVE

HALSEY ST

L BEDFORD AVE

LORIMER ST

GRAND ST

WYCKOFF AVE

WILSON AVE

METROPOLITAN AVE/GRAND ST

MORGAN AVE

KNICKERBOCKER

MONTROSE AVE

J M HEWES ST

BROADWAY LORIMER ST

M CENTRAL AVE

MARCY AVE

FLUSHING AVE

BUSHWICK AVE/ ABERDEEN ST

Z MYRTLE AVE

KOSCIUSKO ST

GATES AVE

HALSEY ST

BROADWAY/ EASTERN PKWY

FLUSHING AVE

CHAUNCEY ST

ROCKAWAY AVE

ATLANTIC AVE

MYRTLE/ WILLOUGHBY

B R O O K L Y N

A C

RALPH AVE

SUTTER AVE

BEDFORD/NOSTRAND

KINGSTON AVE/ THROOP AVE

UTICA AVE

CLASSON AVE

NOSTRAND AVE

ROCKAWAY AVE

G

FULTON ST

FRANKLIN AVE

CLINTON/ WASHINGTON AVE

S

SARATOGA AVE

SUTTER AVE

CONTINUED ON MAP 16

CONTINUED ON MAP 20

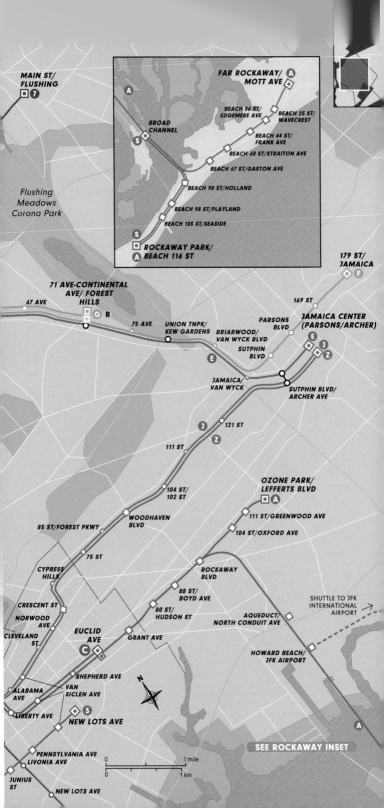

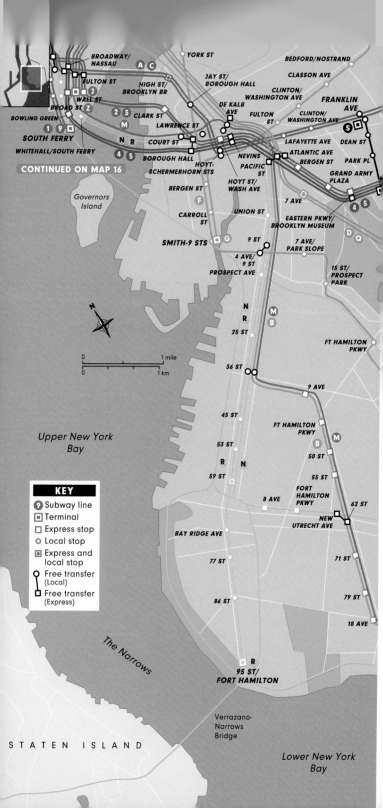

CONTINUED ON MAP 19

Ⓐ Ⓒ
RALPH
AVE
UTICA AVE

SUTTER AVE

VAN SICLEN
AVE
PENNSYLVANIA
AVE
LIVONIA AVE

KINGSTON AVE/
THROOP AVE

JUNIUS ST

NOSTRAND
AVE

SUTTER AVE

③

ROCKAWAY
AVE

NEW LOTS AVE

KINGSTON
AVE

SARATOGA
AVE

E 105 ST

NOSTRAND
AVE

④ UTICA AVE

PRESIDENT ST

Ⓛ CANARSIE/
ROCKAWAY
PKWY

STERLING ST

BOTANIC
GARDEN

WINTHROP ST

Ⓢ PROSPECT
PARK

PARKSIDE
AVE

FRANKLIN
AVE

CHURCH AVE

BEVERLEY RD

CHURCH AVE

NEWKIRK AVE

BEVERLEY
RD

CORTELYOU
RD

② ⑤

CHURCH AVE

NEWKIRK AVE

FLATBUSH AVE/
BROOKLYN
COLLEGE

DITMAS AVE

AVE H

B R O O K L Y N

18 AVE

AVE I

AVE J

Ⓓ Ⓠ

BAY PKWY

Ⓕ

AVE M

AVE N

18 AVE
20 AVE

KINGS HWY

BAY PKWY

AVE P

KINGS HWY

KINGS HWY

AVE U

KINGS HWY

N

AVE U

NECK RD

SHEEPSHEAD
BAY

Ⓜ BAY PKWY

AVE U

20 AVE

25 AVE

86 ST

AVE X

Ⓓ

BAY 50 ST

NEPTUNE AVE/
VAN SICKLEN

BRIGHTON BEACH

Ⓠ

OCEAN PKWY

Rockaway Inlet

Ⓑ Ⓝ

STILLWELL AVE/
CONEY ISLAND

Ⓕ Ⓓ

W 8 ST/
AQUARIUM

Henry
Hudson
Br.

MARBLE
HILL

INWOOD

Dyckman St./
Riverside Dr. S./
The Cloisters

University
Hts. Br.

Grand Concourse

Bronx
River

Bronx
Park

Tremont   Ave.

Dyckman St.

Ft. Tryon Pk./
The Cloisters

FORT
WASHINGTON

181st St.

W. 178th St./
George Washington
Bridge/Riverside Dr./
Cross Bronx Expwy.

Washington
Br.

Hamilton Br.

Cross Bronx Expwy.

THE BRONX

Webster   Ave.

Third   Ave.

Boston   Rd.

W. 158th St./
Riverside
Drive

W. 155th St.

Frederick
Douglass Blvd.

Macombs
Dam Br.

MANHATTANVILLE

E. 161st St.

Melrose   Ave.

Concourse

Hudson   River

Henry Hudson Pkwy.

Riverside Dr.

St. Nicholas Ave.

Broadway

Edgecombe Ave.

Harlem River Dr.

Harlem   River

Major   Deegan

W. 145th St.

W. 138th St.

W. 135th   St.

W. 125th St.

E. 149th St.

145th. St. Br.

Madison
Ave. Br.

3rd Ave. Br.

Willis Ave. Br.

E. 138rd St.

Expwy.

KEY
G 24-hour Gas Station
↱ Northbound Access
↳ Southbound Access

1500 feet

500 meters

W. 125th St.

Riverside
Park

9A

NEW
JERSEY

Amsterdam Ave.

Broadway

Manhattan Ave.

St. Nicholas Ave.

Frederick Douglass Blvd.

Adam Clayton Powell Jr. Blvd.

Lenox Ave./Malcolm X Blvd.

Cathedral Pkwy.

W. 106th St.

Columbus Ave.

Central Park W.

W. 96th St.

UPPER
WEST SIDE

West End Ave.

Riverside Dr.

Central
Park

Harlem
Meer

The
Reservoir

HARLEM

E. 125th St.

E. 116th St.

E. 125th St./
Triborough Br./
Randall's Is.

Randall's
Island

EAST
HARLEM

E. 110th St.

E. 106th St.

E. 96th St.

Fifth Ave.

Madison Ave.

Park Ave.

Lexington Ave.

Third Ave.

Second Ave.

First Ave.

FDR Dr.

Ward's
Island

UPPER
EAST SIDE

York Ave.

E. 96th St.

QUEENS

East   River

W. 96th St.
W. 92nd St.
W. 86th St.

The Reservoir

Central Park

E. 96th St.
E. 92nd St.
E. 86th St.

E. 92nd St.

W. 79th St. Boat Basin

W. 79th St.

The Lake

E. 79th St.

E. 79th St.
Roosevelt Island

LONG ISLAND CITY

W. 72nd St.

W. 72nd St.

UPPER WEST SIDE

The Pond

UPPER EAST SIDE

E. 73rd St.
E. 72nd St.
E. 71st St.

E. 65th St.

9A

Central Park W.

Tenth Ave.

Columbus Ave.

Broadway

Amsterdam Ave.

West End Ave.

Riverside Dr.

West Side Hwy.

Central Park S.
E. 59th St.

E. 63rd St.
E. 61st St.

G

E. 57th St.

Queensboro Bridge

QUEENS

W. 57th St.
W. 55th St.
W. 51st St.
W. 49th St.
W. 47th St.
W. 45th St.
W. 43rd St.
W. 41st St.

G

W. 57th St.
W. 56th St.
W. 54th St.
W. 52nd St.
W. 50th St. W. 50th St.
W. 48th St.
W. 46th St.
W. 44th St.
W. 42nd St.

MIDTOWN

TURTLE BAY

E. 53rd St.
E. 48th St.
E. 47th St.

E. 42nd St.

495

THEATER DISTRICT

Queens-Midtown Tunnel

GREEN-POINT

W. 39 St./Javits Center

E. 37th St.

495

Lincoln Tunnel

W. 34th St.

MURRAY HILL

E. 34th St.

E. 34th St.

W. 30th St.

Eleventh Ave.

Ninth Ave.

Eighth Ave.

Seventh Ave.

Broadway

W. 29th St.

E. 25th St.

W. 26th St.

Ave. of the Americas (Sixth Ave.)

Fifth Ave.

Madison Ave.

Park Ave. S.

Lexington Ave.

Third Ave.

Second Ave.

First Ave.

E. 23rd St.

FDR Dr.

W. 23rd St.

G CHELSEA

GRAMERCY

E. 20th St.

East River

W. 18th St.

W. 14th St.
W. 12th St.

W. 14th St.

E. 14th St.

E. 14th St.

Ave. C

Ave. A
Ave. B
Ave. D

Hudson River

NEW JERSEY

Greenwich Ave.

WEST VILLAGE

Fourth Ave.

GREENWICH VILLAGE

EAST VILLAGE

E. Houston St.

G

HOBOKEN

W. 12th St.

W. 11th St.

Christopher St.

West Side Hwy.

Clarkson St.

W. Houston St.

Varick St.

NOHO

Houston St. G

Bowery

LOWER EAST SIDE

Williamsburg Bridge

SOHO

Broadway

Delancey St.

Grand St.

DOWNTOWN

LITTLE ITALY

Cherry St.

Canal St.

Holland Tunnel

Laight St.

Canal St.

TRIBECA

CHINATOWN

Montgomery St.

Manhattan Bridge

Flatbush Ave.

JERSEY CITY

West Side Hwy.

Chambers St.

Barclay St.

Civic Center

278

Brooklyn Bridge

Vesey St.

Liberty St.

BATTERY PARK CITY

FINANCIAL DISTRICT

SOUTH STREET SEAPORT

BROOKLYN

Brooklyn-Queens Expwy.

Morris St.

Whitehall St.

State St.

Battery Park

N

BROOKLYN HEIGHTS

Brooklyn-Battery Tunnel

NOTE:
West Side south of Chambers St. access on every street

0   1500 feet
0   500 meters

CONTINUED ON MAP 25

W.16th St.
W.15th St.
W.14th St.

Eighth Ave.
Greenwich St.
Seventh Ave. South
Ave. of the Americas

GREENWICH VILLAGE

(Sixth Ave.)

W. 10th St.
Christopher St.

West Side Hwy.

W. Houston St.

Varick St.

Hudson St.

West St.

Canal St.

Holland Tunnel

TRIBECA

N. Moore St.

Harrison St.

Hudson River

Chambers St.

W. Broadway

NEW JERSEY

Vesey St.

X90
9
10

9
10

X90

W. Thames

KEY

	Northbound
	Southbound
	Eastbound
	Westbound
101	Route number
20	Terminal

CONTINUED ON MAP 26

Central Park

W. 72nd St.

W. 70th St.

Amsterdam Ave.

West End Ave.

W. 66th St.
W. 65th St.
W. 60th St.

W. 58th St.
W. 57th St.

Central Park S.

Henry Hudson Pkwy.

9A

72

57

72

66

66

5
7
104

10

7

66
72

66

30

5
7

6

30
57

W. 55th St.
W. 53rd St.

Tenth Ave.

Ninth Ave.

Eighth Ave.

11

11

104
10

6
7

Seventh Ave.

5
6
7

(Sixth Ave.)

Ave. of the Americas

W. 50th St.
W. 49th St.

W. 47th St.

W. 44th St.

Eleventh Ave.

50

50

27

27

104

27

104
10

27
10

W. 42nd St.

42

104

Lincoln Tunnel

50
42

495

42
34

W. 38th St.

W. 36th St.

W. 34th St.

34

27

16

16

10

Broadway

6
7

5
6
7

W. 30th St.

W. 28th St.

W. 25th St.

W. 23rd St.

Ninth Ave.

Eighth Ave.

Seventh Ave.

4

Q32

4
W. 32nd St.

W. 23rd St.

Hudson River

23

CHELSEA

W. 21st St.

W. 18th St.

W. 15th St.

11

11

10

10

5
6
7

14

W. 14th St.

14
10

West Side Hwy.

CONTINUED ON MAP 24

0   1500 feet

0   500 meters

N

MAP 27 Buses/Manhattan above 125th Street

KEY

Northbound
Southbound
Eastbound
Westbound
101 Route number
20 Terminal

Listed Alphabetically

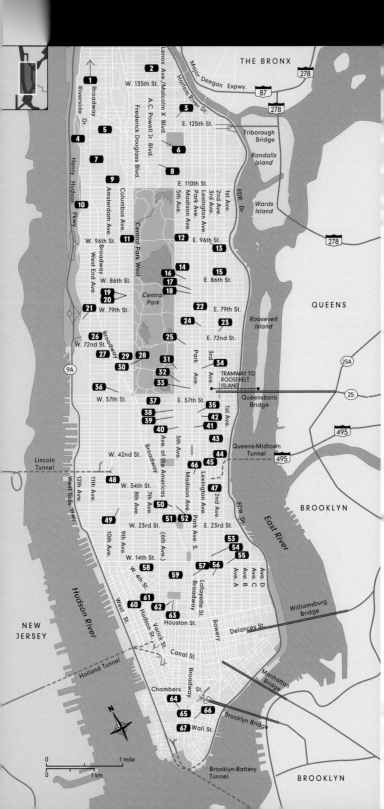

Listed by Site Number

Listed Alphabetically

Listed Alphabetically (cont.)

Church of the UN, 44.
777 UN Plaza ☎ 661-1762.
Inter-Denominational

Congregation Rodeph Sholom, 20.
7 W 83rd ☎ 362-8800. Reform Jewish

Fifth Ave Presbyterian, 38.
Fifth Ave & 55th St ☎ 247-0490

Fifth Ave Synagogue, 32. 5 E 62nd St
☎ 838-2122. Orthodox Jewish

First Church of Christ, Scientist, 11.
1 W 96th St ☎ 749-3088.

Friends Meeting House, 54.
15 Rutherford Pl ☎ 777-8866. Quaker

Grace Church, 57. 802 Broadway
☎ 254-2000. Episcopal

Holy Apostles, 49. 296 Ninth Ave
☎ 807-6799. Episcopal

Holy Family, 43. 315 E 47th St
☎ 753-3401. Roman Catholic

Holy Trinity, 28. Central Park W &
65th St ☎ 877-6815. Lutheran

Holy Trinity Cathedral, 23. 319 E
74th St ☎ 288-3215. Greek Orthodox

Immaculate Conception, 55. 414 E
14th St ☎ 254-0200. Roman Catholic

Islamic Center of NY, 13.
1711 Third Ave ☎ 722-5234. Muslim

James Chapel, 5. 3041 Broadway
☎ 280-1522. Inter-Denominational

John Street United Methodist, 66.
44 John St ☎ 269-0014

Judson Memorial, 62. 55
Washington Sq ☎ 477-0351. Baptist

Marble Collegiate, 50. Fifth Ave &
29th St ☎ 686-2770. Reformed

Masjid Malcolm Shabazz, 8. 102 W
116 St ☎ 662-2200. Muslim

Metropolitan Community, 48.
446 W 36th St ☎ 629-7440. Inter-
denominational/Gay & Lesbian

**Metropolitan-Duane United
Methodist, 58.** 201 W 13th St
☎ 243-5470.

NY Buddhist Temple, 10.
332 Riverside Dr ☎ 678-0305

Park Ave Christian, 17. 1010 Park
Ave ☎ 288-3246. Disciples of Christ

Park Ave Synagogue, 16. 50 E 87th
St ☎ 369-2600. Conservative Jewish

Riverside, 4. Riverside Dr & 120th
☎ 870-6700. Inter-Denominational

Rutgers Presbyterian, 26.
236 W 73rd St ☎ 877-8227.

St Andrew's, 3. Fifth Ave & 127th St
☎ 534-0896. Episcopal

St Bartholomew's, 42. 109 E 50th St
☎ 378-0200. Episcopal

St Ignatius Loyola, 18. 980 Park Ave
☎ 288-3588. Roman Catholic

St James, 25. 865 Madison Ave
☎ 288-4100. Episcopal

St John's Lutheran, 61.
81 Christopher St ☎ 242-5737

St Mark's-in-the-Bowery, 56. Second
Ave & 10th St ☎ 674-6377. Episcopal

St Martin's Episcopal, 6.
230 Lenox Ave ☎ 534-4531

St Matthew & St Timothy, 19.
26 W 84th St ☎ 362-6750. Episcopal

St Nicholas Russian Orthodox, 12.
15 E 97th St ☎ 289-1915.

St Patrick's Cathedral, 40. Fifth Ave
& 50th St ☎ 753-2261. Roman Cath

St Paul the Apostle, 36. 415 W 59th
St ☎ 265-3209. Roman Catholic

St Paul's Chapel, 65. Broadway &
Fulton St ☎ 602-0874. Episcopal

St Paul's Chapel, 7. Columbia Univ,
Broadway & 117th St ☎ 854-6625.
Inter-Denominational

St Peter's, 64. 16 Barclay St
☎ 233-8355. Roman Catholic

St Peter's, 41. 619 Lexington Ave
☎ 935-2200. Lutheran

St Thomas, 39. 1 W 53rd St
☎ 757-7013. Episcopal

St Vartan Armenian Cathedral, 47.
630 Second Ave ☎ 686-0710.
Armenian Orthodox

St Vincent Ferrer, 34.
Lexington Ave & 66th St ☎ 744-2080.
Roman Catholic

Stephen Wise Free Synagogue, 29.
30 W 68th St ☎ 877-4050.
Reform Jewish

Temple Emanu-El, 31.
1 E 65th St ☎ 744-1400.
Reform Jewish

Trinity, 67. 74 Trinity Pl
☎ 602-0800. Episcopal

**Washington Square United
Methodist, 63.** 135 W 4th St
☎ 777-2528.

West End Collegiate, 21. 368 West
End Ave ☎ 787-1566. Reformed

West End Synagogue, 22. 190
Amsterdam Ave ☎ 579-0777.
Reconstructionist Jewish

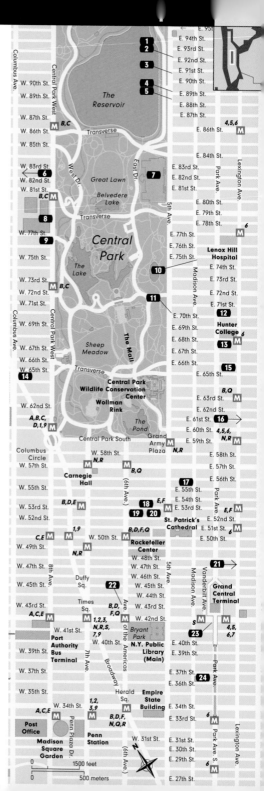

MAP **31** **Museums/Elsewhere in Manhattan**

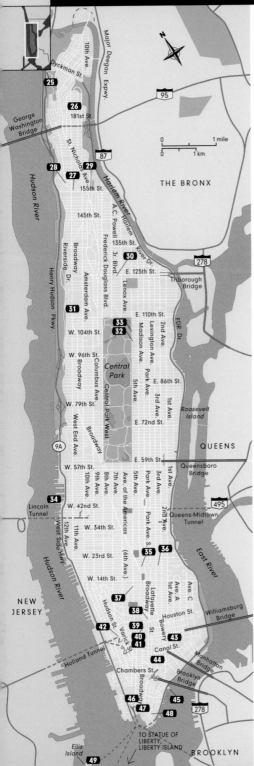

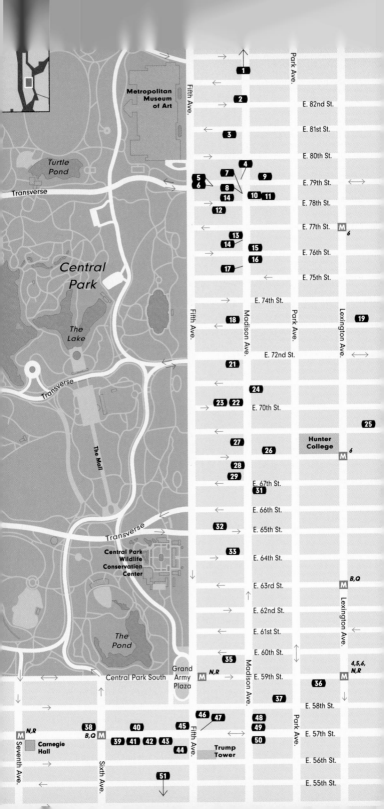

E. 84th St.
E. 83rd St.

Third Ave.
Second Ave.
First Ave.

E. 73rd St.
20
E. 72nd St.
E. 71st St.
E. 70th St.
E. 69th St.
E. 68th St.
30

Third Ave.
Second Ave.
First Ave.

0   600 feet
0   200 meters

34 TRAMWAY TO ROOSEVELT ISLAND
Queensboro Bridge

Third Ave.
Second Ave.
First Ave.

N

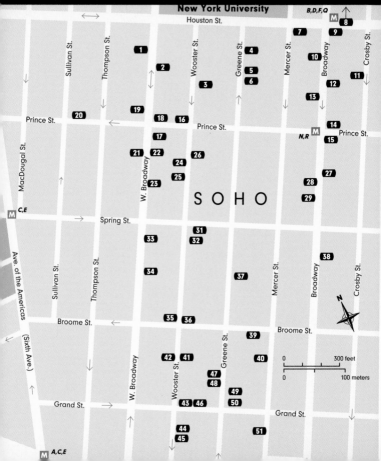

Art Galleries/SoHo

Chelsea Galleries
Listed Alphabetically

AC Project Room, 21.
453 W 17th St ☎ 645–4970

Barbara Gladstone, 7.
515 W 24th St ☎ 206–9300

Cheim & Reid, 8. 521 W 23rd St
☎ 242–7727

Clementine, 2. 526 W 26th St
☎ 243–5937

D'Amelio Terras, 12. 525 W 22nd St
☎ 352–9460

Dia Center for the Arts, 16.
548 W 22nd St ☎ 989–5566

Greene Naftali, 2. 526 W 26th St
☎ 463–7770

Henry Urbach Architecture, 14.
526 W 22nd St ☎ 627–0974

Jessica Fredericks, 11. 504 W 22nd St
☎ 633–6555.

Kreps, 18. 529 W 20th St ☎ 741–8849

Linda Kirkland, 11. 504 W 22nd St
☎ 627–3930

Luhring Augustine, 4. 531 W 24th St
☎ 206–9100

Matthew Marks, 5. 523 W 24th St
☎ 243–0200

Matthew Marks, 13. 522 W 22nd St
☎ 243–1650

Max Protech, 10.
511 W 22nd St ☎ 633–6999

Maynes, 18. 529 W 20th St
☎ 741–3318.

Metro Pictures, 6. 519 W 24th St
☎ 206–7100

Morthland, 9. 225 Tenth Ave
☎ 242–7767

Pat Hearn, 15. 530 W 22nd St
☎ 727–7366.

Paula Cooper, 17. 534 W 21st St
☎ 255–1105

Postmasters, 20. 459 W 19th St
☎ 727–3323

Ricco Maresca, 18. 529 W 20th St
☎ 627–4819

Shainman, 19. 513 W 20th St
☎ 645–1701

Robert Mann, 3. 210 11th Ave
☎ 989–7600

Team, 1. 527 W 26th St ☎ 279–9219

303, 12. 525 W 22nd St ☎ 255–1121

XL, 11. 504 W 22nd St ☎ 462–4111.

Soho Galleries
Listed Alphabetically

American Fine Arts, 44.
22 Wooster St ☎ 941–0401

American Primitive, 9.
594 Broadway ☎ 966–1530

Amos Eno, 9.
594 Broadway ☎ 226–5342

Artists Space, 50.
38 Greene St ☎ 226–3970

Atlantic, 41.
40 Wooster St ☎ 219–3183

Basilico Fine Arts, 45.
26 Wooster St ☎ 966–1831

Brooke Alexander, 35.
59 Wooster St ☎ 925–4338

Bruce R Lewin, 18.
136 Prince St ☎ 431–4750

Charles Cowles, 21.
420 W Broadway ☎ 925–3500

Curt Marcus, 12. 578 Broadway
☎ 226–3200

David Zwirner, 47. 43 Greene St
☎ 966–9074

Deitch Projects, 46. 76 Grand St
☎ 343–7300

Dia Center for the Arts, 33.
393 W Broadway
☎ 989–5566

Dia Center for the Arts, 16.
141 Wooster St ☎ 989–5566

The Drawing Center, 42.
35 Wooster St ☎ 219–2166

Dyansen of Soho, 1.
462 W Broadway ☎ 982-3668

EM Donahue, 15.
560 Broadway ☎ 226–1111

Emily Harvey, 28.
537 Broadway ☎ 925–7651

Exit Art, 27. 548 Broadway
☎ 966–7745

Feature, 37. 76 Greene St
☎ 941–7077

55 Mercer, 40. 55 Mercer St
☎ 226–8513

First St, 15. 560 Broadway
☎ 226–9127

Gagosian, 3.
136 Wooster St ☎ 228–2828

Gallery 292, 26.
120 Wooster St ☎ 431–0292

Henoch Gallery, 32.
80 Wooster St ☎ 966–0303

Holly Solomon, 7. 172 Mercer St
☎ 941-5777

Howard Greenberg, 26.
120 Wooster St ☎ 334-0010

Howard Schickler, 15. 560 Broadway
☎ 431-6363

John Gibson, 14. 568 Broadway
☎ 925-1192

June Kelly, 10. 591 Broadway
☎ 226-1660

Kaplan, 49.
48 Greene St ☎ 226-6131

Lehmann Maupin, 48.
39 Greene St ☎ 965-0753

Leica, 8. 670 Broadway
☎ 777-3051

Lennon, Weinberg, 15.
560 Broadway ☎ 941-0012

Meisel, 20. 141 Prince St ☎ 677-1340

Nancy Hoffman, 22.
429 W Broadway ☎ 966-6676

OK Harris, 34. 383 W Broadway
☎ 431-3600

Pace Wildenstein, 4. 142 Greene St
☎ 431-9224

Paul Kasmin, 43. 74 Grand St
☎ 219-3219

Penine Hart, 37. 457 Broome St
☎ 226-2761

Peter Blum, 25. 99 Wooster St
☎ 343-0441

Phoenix, 14. 568 Broadway
☎ 226-8711

Phyllis Kind, 5. 136 Greene St
☎ 925-1200

PPOW, 36. 476 Broome St
☎ 941-8642

Reusch, 31. 134 Spring St
☎ 925-1137

Richardson, 15. 560 Broadway
☎ 343-1255

Ronald Feldman, 51. 31 Mercer St
☎ 226-3232

Sally Hawkins, 19. 448 W Broadway
☎ 477-5699

Sandra Gering, 36. 476 Broome St
☎ 226-8195

SoHo 20, 29.
545 Broadway ☎ 226-4167

Solo Impression, 38. 520
Broadway ☎ 925-3599

Sonnabend, 21. 420 W Broadway
☎ 966-6160

Sperone Westwater, 4.
142 Greene St ☎ 431-3685

Sragow, 30. 73 Spring St ☎ 219-1793

Staley-Wise, 15.
560 Broadway ☎ 966-6223

Stark, 11. 113 Crosby St
☎ 925-4484

Steinbaum Krauss, 6.
132 Greene St ☎ 431-4224

Stephen Haller, 15.
560 Broadway ☎ 219-2500

Susan Teller, 14.
568 Broadway ☎ 941-7335

Tenri, 13. 575 Broadway
☎ 925-8500

Tony Shafrazi, 24.
119 Wooster St ☎ 274-9300

Vorpal, 2. 459 W Broadway
☎ 777-3939

Ward-Nasse, 20. 178 Prince St
☎ 925-6951

Witkin, 23. 415 W Broadway
☎ 925-5510

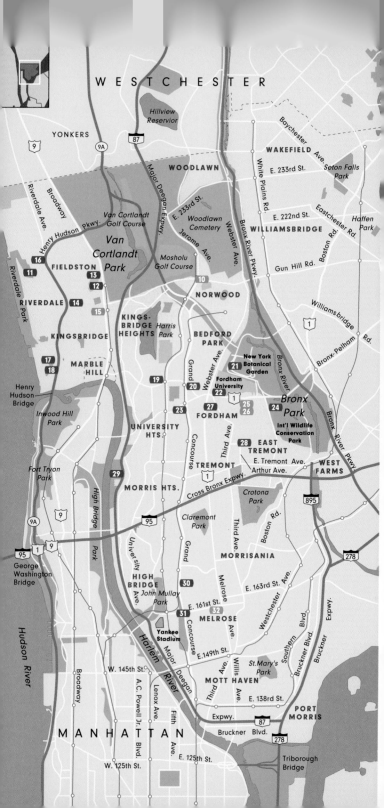

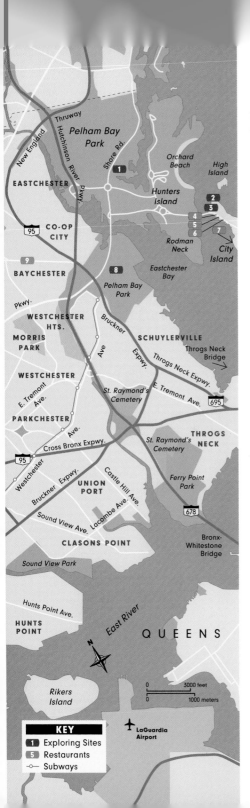

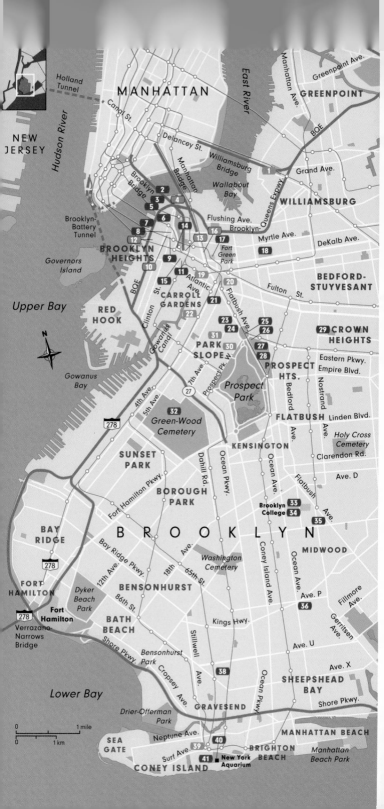

Staten Island Listed by Site Number

BRONX SITES

Arthur Ave Italian Market, 28. Arthur Ave, betw E Fordham Rd & E Tremont Ave

Bartow-Pell Mansion, 1. Shore Rd & Pelham Bay Pkwy ☎ 718/885-1461

Bronx County Courthouse, 31. 851 Grand Concourse ☎ 718/590-3640

Bronx Museum of the Arts, 30. 1040 Grand Concourse ☎ 718/681-6000

Bronx Zoo (IWCP), 24. Fordham Rd & Southern Blvd ☎ 718/367-1010

Christ Church, 16. Henry Hudson Pkwy & 252nd St

City Island, 2. Long Island Sound

Creston Ave Baptist Church, 23. 114 E 188th St ☎ 718/367-1754

Edgar Allan Poe Cottage, 20. Grand Concourse & E Kingsbridge Rd ☎ 718/881-8900

Edgehill Church, 18. 2570 Independence Ave ☎ 718/549-7324

Enrico Fermi Cultural Center/Library, 27. 610 E 186th St ☎ 718/933-6410

Fordham University, 22. 441 E Fordham Rd ☎ 718/817-1000

Henry Hudson Memorial, 17. Independence Ave & W 227th St

Kingsbridge Armory, 19. Kingsbridge Rd & Jerome Ave

Manhattan College, 13. Manhattan College Pkwy & W 242nd St ☎ 718/862-8000

North Wind Undersea Museum, 3. 610 City Island Ave ☎ 718/885-0701

NY Botanical Garden, 21. Southern Blvd & 200th St ☎ 718/817-8500

Pelham Bay Park, 8. Pelham Bay

Roberto Clemente State Park, 29. W Tremont Ave & Matthewson Rd ☎ 718/299-8750

Van Cortlandt House Museum, 12. B'way & W 246th St ☎ 718/543-3344

Wave Hill, 11. 249th St & Independence Ave. ☎ 718/549-3200

World War I Memorial Tower, 14. Riverdale Ave & 239th St

BRONX RESTAURANTS

Alex & Henry's Restaurant, 32. 862 Cortlandt Ave ☎ 718/585-3290. Italian. $

Amici's Italian Restaurant, 4. 566 E 187th St ☎ 718/364-8598. Italian. $$

Ann & Tony's Restaurant, 25. 2407 Arthur Ave ☎ 718/364-8250. Italian. $$

Dominick's, 26. 2335 Arthur Ave ☎ 718/733-2807. Italian. $$

Il Boschetto Finest Italian, 9. 1660 E Gun Hill Rd ☎ 718/379-9335. Italian. $$

King Lobster, 6. 500 City Island Ave ☎ 718/885-1579. Seafood. $$

Portofino Restaurant, 5. 555 City Island Ave ☎ 718/885-1220. Continental. $$

Riverdale Diner, 15. 3657 Kingsbridge Ave ☎ 718/884-6050. Diner. $

Sammy's Fish Box, 7. 41 City Island Ave ☎ 718/885-0920. Seafood. $$

Sincere Garden, 10. 89 E Gun Hill Rd ☎ 718/882-5923. Chinese. $$

BROOKLYN SITES

Bargemusic, Ltd, 5. Fulton Ferry Landing, Old Fulton St & Waterfront ☎ 718/624-4061

Bklyn Acad of Music (BAM), 21. 30 Lafayette Ave ☎ 718/636-4100

Bklyn Borough Hall, 14. 209 Joralemon St

Bklyn Botanic Garden, 28. 900 Washington Ave ☎ 718/623-7200

Bklyn Bridge, 2. Cadman Plaza, Bklyn, to City Hall Park, Manhattan

Bklyn Center of Performing Arts, 34. Brooklyn College, Bedford & H Aves ☎ 718/951-4500

Bklyn Children's Museum, 29. 145 Brooklyn Ave ☎ 718/735-4432

Bklyn College CUNY, 33. Bedford & H Aves ☎ 718/951-5000

MAP **35**

$$$$ = *over $60* $$$ = *$40-$59* $$ = *$20-$39* $ = *under $20*

Based on cost per person, excluding drinks, service, and 8¼% sales tax.

MAP 36

QUEENS SITES (cont.)

Queens Botanical Gardens, 25.
43-50 Main St ☎ 718/886-3800

Queens Historical Society, 21.
143-35 37th Ave ☎ 718/939-0647

Queens Museum, 19. Flushing
Meadows-Corona Park ☎ 718/592-5555

Silvercup Studios, 3. 42-25 21st St
☎ 718/784-3390

St Demitrios, 11. 30-11 30th Dr
☎ 718/728-1718

St John's University, 28.
Grand Central & Utopia Pkwys
☎ 718/990-6161

Weeping Beech Tree, 24.
37th Ave & Parsons Blvd

West Side Tennis Club, 27.
1 Tennis Pl ☎ 718/268-2300

QUEENS RESTAURANTS

Café Vernon, 2. 46-18 Vernon
Blvd ☎ 718/472-9694. Italian. $$

Elias Corner, 12. 31st St & 24th Ave
☎ 718/932-1510. Seafood. $$

Jai-Ya Thai, 16. 81-11 Broadway
☎ 718/651-1330. Thai. $

Karyatis, 9. 35-03 Broadway
☎ 718/204-0666. Greek. $$

Jackson Diner, 14. 37-47 74th St
☎ 718/672-1232. Indian. $

Park Side, 17. 107-01 Corona Ave
☎ 718/271-9274. Italian. $$

Piccola Venezia, 13. 42-01 28th Ave
☎ 718/721-8470. Italian. $$-$$$

Tierras Columbianas, 15. 82-18
Roosevelt Ave ☎ 718/426-8868.
Colombian. $

Water's Edge Restaurant, 1.
44th Dr at East River ☎ 718/482-0033.
American. $$$

STATEN ISLAND SITES

Alice Austin House, 8. 2 Hylan Blvd
☎ 718/816-4506

Garibaldi-Meucci Museum, 7.
420 Tompkins Ave ☎ 718/442-1608

**Gateway National Recreation
Area, 12.** Fort Wadsworth
☎ 718/338-3338

**Historic Richmondtown/Staten
Island Historical Society, 11.**
441 Clarke Ave ☎ 718/351-1611

**Jacques Marchais Museum of
Tibetan Art, 10.** 338 Lighthouse Ave
☎ 718/987-3500

Museum of Staten Island, 2. 75
Stuyvesant Pl ☎ 718/727-1135

Snug Harbor Cultural Center, 4.
1000 Richmond Ter ☎ 718/448-2500

Staten Island Botanical Garden, 4.
1000 Richmond Terrace
☎ 718/273-8200

Staten Island Ferry, 1. St George
Station, Richmond Terrace & Hyatt St
☎ 718/815-2628

Staten Island Institute, 3.
75 Stuyvesant Pl ☎ 718/727-1135

Staten Island Zoo, 5. 614
Broadway ☎ 718/442-3100

STATEN ISLAND RESTAURANTS

Angelina's, 15. 26 Jefferson
Blvd ☎ 718/227-7100. Italian. $$

Arirang, 14. 23A Nelson Ave
☎ 718/966-9600. Japanese. $$$

Denino's Pizzeria, 9. 524 Port
Richmond Ave ☎ 718/442-9406.
Pizza. $

Marina Cafe, 13. 154 Mansion Ave
☎ 718/967-3077. American. $$

Real Madrid, 6. 2075 Forest Ave
☎ 718/447-7885. Spanish. $$

MAP **37**

$$$$ = over $60 $$$ = $40-$59 $$ = $20-$39 $ = under $20
Based on cost per person, excluding drinks, service, and 8¼% sales tax.

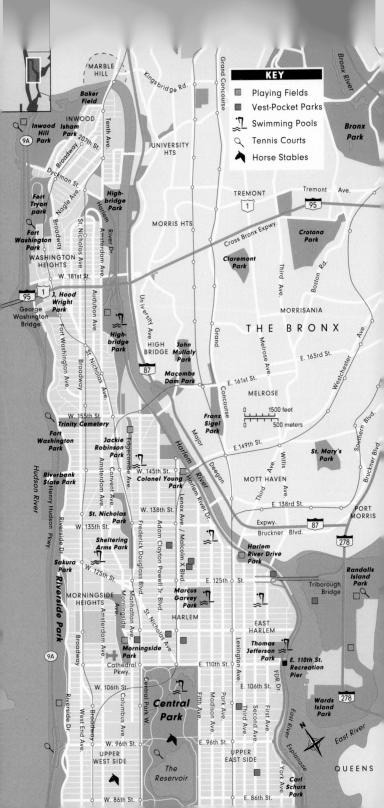

Parks/

Riverside Park

West 86th St.
West End Ave.
Riverside Dr.
W. 86th St.
W. 79th St.
Amsterdam Ave.
Broadway
W. 72nd St.
Columbus Ave.
Central Park W.

Theodore Roosevelt Park

Central Park

The Reservoir

UPPER WEST SIDE

The Lake

Children's Zoo

Central Park Wildlife Conservation Center

Damrosch Park

9A

W. 57th St.

Central Park S.

The Pond

DeWitt Clinton Park

Ninth Ave.
Eighth Ave.
Tenth Ave.
W. 50th St.

Eleventh Ave.

THEATER DISTRICT

Lincoln Tunnel

W. 42nd St.

Bryant Park

495

HELL'S KITCHEN

W. 34th St.

Ninth Ave.
Eighth Ave.
Seventh Ave.
Tenth Ave.

Chelsea Park

W. 23rd St.

Ave. of the Americas

CHELSEA

Madison Square Park

W. 14th St.

Union Square Park

Greenwich Ave.

Jefferson Market Garden

GREENWICH VILLAGE

WEST VILLAGE

Washington Ave.

Washington Square Park

J.J. Walker Park

Hudson River

Hudson St.
Varick St.
Greenwich St.
West Side Hwy.

SOHO

Houston St.

Bowery

Broadway

TRIBECA

Canal St.
Church St.

LITTLE ITALY

Chambers St.

CHINATOWN

Columbus Park

Gov. Smith Park

Holland Tunnel

NEW JERSEY

HOBOKEN

North Park

City Hall Park

FINANCIAL DISTRICT

BATTERY PARK CITY

Robert F. Wagner Jr. Park

Battery Park

Wall St.

Brooklyn-Battery Tunnel

E. 86th St.

Carl Shurz Park

John Jay Park

E. 79th St.
E. 72nd St.
Lexington Ave.
Park Ave.
Madison Ave.
Fifth Ave.
Third Ave.
Second Ave.
First Ave.
York Ave.
FDR Dr.

East River Esplanade

Roosevelt Island

UPPER EAST SIDE

E. 65th St.

E. 59th St.

TRAMWAY

Queensboro Bridge

E. 57th St.

LONG ISLAND CITY

QUEENS

E. 53rd St.

E. 42nd St.

Queens-Midtown Tunnel

St. Vartan's Park

MURRAY HILL

E. 34th St.

Madison Ave.
Park Ave.
Fifth Ave.
Lexington Ave.
Third Ave.
Second Ave.
First Ave.

BROOKLYN

East River

E. 23rd St.

Gramercy Park

GRAMERCY

Stuyvesant Square Park

E. 14th St.

Ave. A
Ave. B
Ave. C
Ave. D

EAST VILLAGE

Tompkins Square Park

East River Park

Fourth Ave.
Lafayette

E. Houston St.

LOWER EAST SIDE

Sara D. Roosevelt Park

Williamsburg Bridge

Corlears Hook Park

Broadway

Seward Park

Manhattan Bridge

278

Flatbush Ave.

Brooklyn Bridge

BROOKLY

BROOKLYN HEIGHTS

Brooklyn-Queens Expwy.

Adams St.

Joralemon St.

1500 feet

500 meters

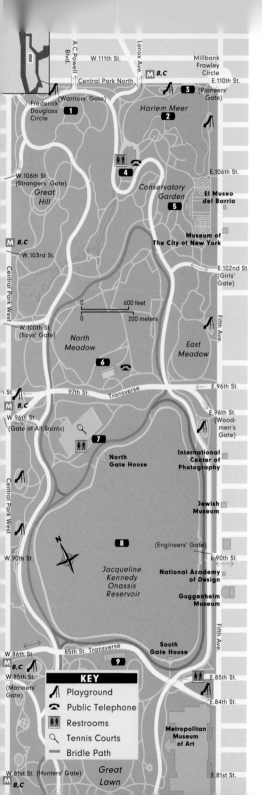

A.C. Powell Blvd.
W.111th St.
Lenox Ave.
Central Park North
Millbank Frawley Circle
E.110th St.
M B,C
(Warriors' Gate)
Frederick Douglass Circle
1
(Pioneers' Gate)
3
Harlem Meer
2
W.106th St. (Strangers' Gate)
Great Hill
4
E.106th St.
Conservatory Garden
5
El Museo del Barrio
M B,C
W.103rd St.
Museum of The City of New York
Central Park West
E.102nd St. (Girls' Gate)
600 feet
200 meters
W.100th St. (Boys' Gate)
North Meadow
6
East Meadow
Fifth Ave.
97th St. Transverse
E.96th St.
M B,C
W.96th St. (Gate of All Saints)
E.96th St. (Wood-men's Gate)
7
North Gate House
International Center of Photography
Jewish Museum
(Engineers' Gate)
8
Central Park West
E.90th St.
W.90th St.
Jacqueline Kennedy Onassis Reservoir
National Academy of Design
Guggenheim Museum
Fifth Ave.
South Gate House
W.86th St.
85th St. Transverse
M B,C
9
W.85th St. (Mariners' Gate)
E.85th St.
E.84th St.

KEY
- 🛝 Playground
- ☎ Public Telephone
- 🚻 Restrooms
- 🔍 Tennis Courts
- — Bridle Path

Metropolitan Museum of Art

W.81st St. (Hunters' Gate)
M B,C
Great Lawn
E.81st St.

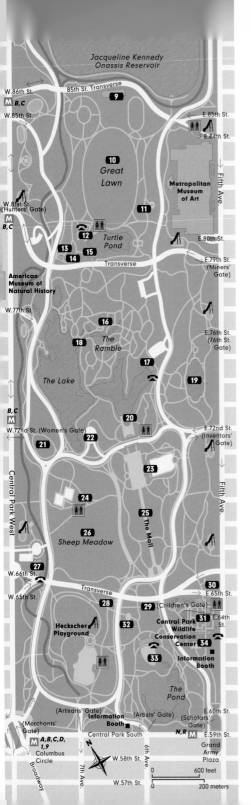

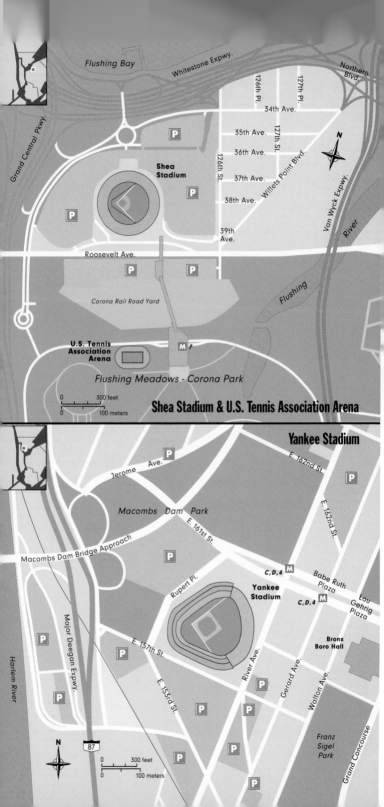

Shea Stadium & U.S. Tennis Association Arena

Yankee Stadium

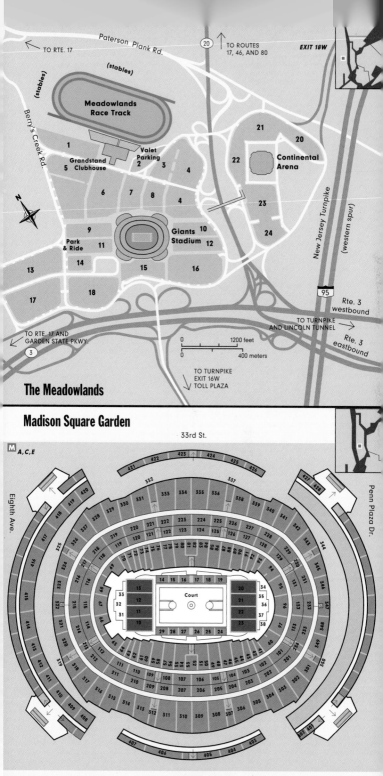

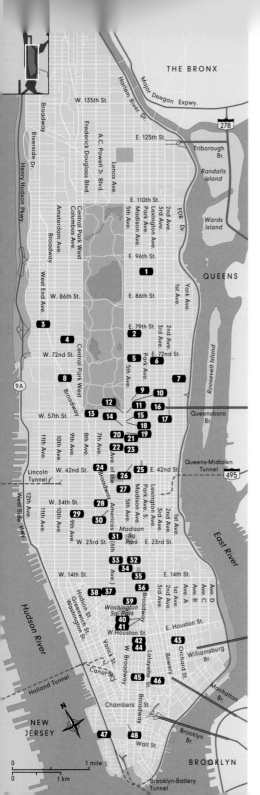

MAP 43

Listed Alphabetically

ABC Carpet & Home, 32.
881 & 888 Broadway ☎ 473-3000

B&H Photo-Video, 29.
420 Ninth Ave ☎ 444-5045

Balducci's, 37.
424 Sixth Ave ☎ 673-2600

Barneys NY, 9.
660 Madison Ave ☎ 826-8900

Bed, Bath & Beyond, 33.
620 Sixth Ave ☎ 255-3550

Bergdorf Goodman, 12.
754 Fifth Ave ☎ 753-7300

Bloomingdale's, 16.
1000 Third Ave ☎ 355-5900

Brooks Brothers, 26.
346 Madison Ave ☎ 682-8800

Century 21, 48.
22 Cortlandt St ☎ 227-9092

Crate & Barrel, 10.
650 Madison Ave ☎ 308-0011

Dean & Deluca, 44. 560 Broadway
☎ 431-1691

FAO Schwarz, 11.
767 Fifth Ave ☎ 644-9400

Fortunoff, 19.
681 Fifth Ave ☎ 758-6660

Grace's Marketplace, 6.
1237 Third Ave ☎ 737-0600

Grand Central Terminal Shops, 25.
Park Ave & 42nd St

Henri Bendel, 14.
712 Fifth Ave ☎ 247-1100

Kalustyan's, 30. 123 Lexington Ave
☎ 685-3451

Kate's Paperie, 42. 561 Broadway
☎ 941-9816

Kitchen Arts & Letters, 1.
1435 Lexington Ave ☎ 876-5550

Lord & Taylor, 27.
424 Fifth Ave ☎ 391-3344

Macy's, 28. Herald Sq &
34th St ☎ 695-4400

Maison du Chocolat, 2.
1018 Madison Ave ☎ 744-7117

Manhattan Art & Antiques Center, 17.
1050 Second Ave ☎ 355-4400

**Museum of Modern Art
Design Store, 20.**
44 W 53rd St ☎ 767-1050

Paragon, 34.
867 Broadway ☎ 255-8036

Patricia Field, 39. 10 E Eighth St
☎ 254-1699

Pearl Paint, 45. 308 Canal St
☎ 431-7932

Pearl River, 46. 277 Canal St
☎ 431-4770

Petrossian, 13. 182 W 58th St
☎ 245-2217

Polo/Polo Sport, 5.
867 Madison Ave ☎ 606-2100;
888 Madison Ave ☎ 434-8000

Rockefeller Center, 22.
30 Rockefeller Plaza ☎ 632-3975

Saks Fifth Ave, 23. 611 Fifth Ave
☎ 753-4000

Strand Books, 36. 828 Broadway
☎ 473-1452

Takashimaya, 21. 693 Fifth Ave
☎ 350-0100

Tiffany & Co, 15. 727 Fifth Ave
☎ 755-8000

Tower Records, 8. 1966 Broadway
☎ 799-2500

Tower Records, 41. 692 Broadway
☎ 505-1500

Trump Tower, 18. 725 Fifth Ave
☎ 832-2000

Virgin Megastore, 24. 1540
Broadway ☎ 921-1020

World Financial Center, 47.
Waterfront, at West & Vesey Sts
☎ 945-0505

Zabar's, 3. 2245 Broadway
☎ 787-2000

MARKETS

**Annex Antiques Fair & Flea
Market, 31.** Sixth Ave, betw 25th &
26th Sts. Open Sat, Sun

Orchard St, 43. Orchard St, betw
Houston & Canal Sts

PS 183 Market, 7. 67th St betw York &
First Aves. Open Sat

PS 41 Market, 38. Greenwich Ave &
Charles St. Open Sat

IS 44 Market, 4. Columbus Ave betw
76th & 77th Sts. Open Sun

Tower Market, 40. B'way betw W 4th
& Great Jones Sts. Open Sat, Sun

Union Square Greenmarket, 35.
Union Sq & 14th St. Open Wed, Fri, Sat

MAP 44 Shopping/Madison Avenue

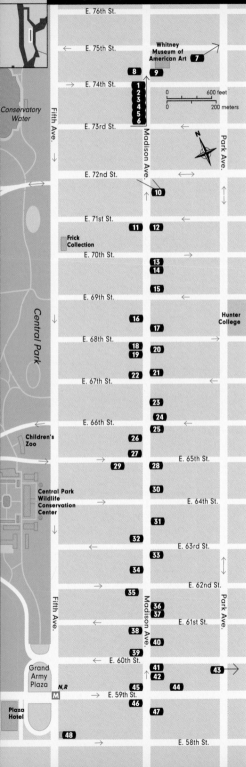

Listed Alphabetically

Ann Taylor, 41.
645 Madison Ave ☎ 832–2010

Archiva, 8.
944 Madison Ave ☎ 439–9194

Baccarat, 47.
625 Madison Ave ☎ 826–4100

Bally of Switzerland, 46.
628 Madison Ave ☎ 751–9082

Barnes & Noble, 7.
86th & Lexington Ave. ☎ 423–9900

Barneys NY, 38.
660 Madison Ave ☎ 826–8900

Billy Martin's, 18.
810 Madison Ave ☎ 861–3100

Bottega Veneta, 42.
635 Madison Ave ☎ 371–5511

Calvin Klein, 39.
654 Madison Ave ☎ 292–9000

Christian Louboutin, 9.
941 Madison Ave ☎ 396-1884

Christofle, 35.
680 Madison Ave ☎ 308–9390

Coach Store, 32.
710 Madison Ave ☎ 319–1772

Crate & Barrel, 45.
650 Madison Ave. ☎ 308–0011

Diesel, 43.
770 Lexington Ave. ☎ 308–0055

DKNY, 40.
655 Madison Ave ☎ 223–3569

Dolce & Gabbana, 21.
825 Madison Ave ☎ 249–4100

E Braun & Co, 31.
717 Madison Ave ☎ 838–0650

EAT, 2.
1064 Madison Ave. ☎ 772–0022

Emanuel Ungaro, 22.
792 Madison Ave ☎ 249–4090

Erica Wilson, 31.
717 Madison Ave ☎ 832–7290

FAO Schwarz, 48.
767 Fifth Ave ☎ 644–9400

Fred Leighton, 25.
773 Madison Ave ☎ 288–1872

Georg Jensen, 36.
683 Madison Ave ☎ 759–6457

Gianni Versace, 17.
815 Madison Ave ☎ 744–6868

Giorgio Armani, 27.
760 Madison Ave ☎ 988–9191

Issey Miyake, 6.
992 Madison Ave ☎ 439–7822

Joan & David, 16.
816 Madison Ave ☎ 772–3970

Julie Artisans' Gallery, 26.
762 Madison Ave ☎ 717–5959

Krizia, 24.
769 Madison Ave ☎ 879–1211

La Maison du Chocolat, 3.
1018 Madison Ave ☎ 744–7117

La Perla, 23.
777 Madison Ave ☎ 570–0050

Madison Ave Bookshop, 14.
833 Madison Ave ☎ 535–6130

Missoni, 4.
1009 Madison Ave ☎ 517–9339

Mitchel London Foods, 29.
22A E 65th St ☎ 737–2850

Moschino, 20.
803 Madison Ave. ☎ 639–6900

Peress, 30.
739 Madison Ave. ☎ 861–6336

Peter Fox, 19.
806 Madison Ave ☎ 744–8340

Pierre Deux, 11.
870 Madison Ave ☎ 570–9343

Polo/Polo Sport, 10.
867 Madison Ave ☎ 606–2100 and
888 Madison Ave ☎ 434–8000

Prada, 13.
841 Madison Ave ☎ 327–4200

Pratesi, 15.
829 Madison Ave ☎ 288–2315

Sherry Lehmann Inc, 37.
679 Madison Ave ☎ 838–7500

Simon Pearce, 43.
500 Park Ave. ☎ 421–8801

Suzanne, 34.
700 Madison Ave. 593–3232

Timberland, 33.
709 Madison Ave ☎ 754–0436

Valentino, 28.
747 Madison Ave ☎ 772–6969

Vera Wang, 4.
991 Madison Ave ☎ 628–3400

Wicker Garden's Baby, 1.
1327 Madison Ave ☎ 410–7001

Yves St Laurent, 12.
855 Madison Ave ☎ 472–5299

MAP 45 Shopping/Fifth Avenue & 57th Street

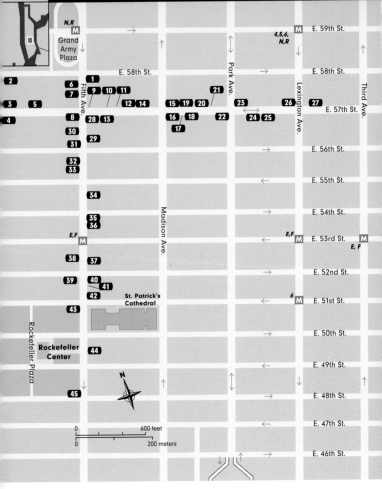

Listed Alphabetically

Barnes & Noble, 45. 600 Fifth Ave
☎ 765-0590

Bergdorf Goodman, 3. 754 Fifth Ave
☎ 753-7300

Borders, 23.
461 Park Ave ☎ 980-6785

Brooks Brothers, 38.
666 Fifth Ave ☎ 261-9440

Buccellati, 18. 46 E 57th St
☎ 308-5533

Bulgari, 8. 730 Fifth Ave ☎ 315-9000

Burberrys, 11. 9 E 57th St ☎ 371-5010

Cartier, 40. 653 Fifth Ave ☎ 753-0111

Chanel, 14. 15 E 57th St ☎ 355-5050

Coach, 15.
595 Madison Ave ☎ 754-0041

Coliseum, 3.
1771 Broadway ☎ 757-8381

Daffy's, 26. 125 E 57th St ☎ 376-4477

Dana Buchman, 21. 65 E 57th St
☎ 319-3257

Dempsey & Carroll, 24. 110 E 57th St
☎ 486-7526

Dunhill, 22. 450 Park Ave
☎ 753-9292

Fendi, 31. 720 Fifth Ave ☎ 767-0100

Fortunoff, 36. 681 Fifth Ave
☎ 758-6660

Gazebo, 25. 114 E 57th St
☎ 832-7077

Gianni Versace Boutique, 42.
647 Fifth Ave ☎ 317-0224

Gucci, 35. 685 Fifth Ave ☎ 826-2600

H Stern, 41. 645 Fifth Ave
☎ 688-0300

Hammacher Schlemmer, 27.
147 E 57th St ☎ 421-9000

Harry Winston, 32. 718 Fifth Ave
☎ 245-2000

Henri Bendel, 33. 712 Fifth Ave
☎ 247-1100

Hermès, 12. 11 E 57th St
☎ 751-3181

Lee's Art Shop, 4. 220 W 57th St
☎ 247-0110

Liz Claiborne, 39. 650 Fifth Ave
☎ 956-6505

Louis Vuitton, 20. 49 E 57th St
☎ 371-6111

Mikimoto, 8. 730 Fifth Ave
☎ 664-1800

NBA Store, 38. 666 Fifth Ave
☎ 515-6221

NikeTown, 13. 6 E 57th St
☎ 891-6453

Petrossian, 2. 182 W 58th St
☎ 245-2217

Prada, 19. 45 E 57th St ☎ 308-2332

Prada, 30. 724 Fifth Ave ☎ 664-0010

Rizzoli, 5. 31 W 57th St
☎ 759-2424

Saks Fifth Ave, 44. 611 Fifth Ave
☎ 753-4000

Salvatore Ferragamo Women's, 37.
661 Fifth Ave ☎ 759-3822

Salvatore Ferragamo Men's, 29.
725 Fifth Ave ☎ 759-7990

Sephora, 43. 636 Fifth Ave
☎ 245-1633

Swatch, 10. 5 E 57th St ☎ 317-1100

Takashimaya, 34. 693 Fifth Ave.
☎ 350-0100

Tiffany & Co, 28. 727 Fifth Ave
☎ 755-8000

Tootsi Plohound, 17.
38 E 57th St ☎ 231-3199

Trump Tower, 29.
725 Fifth Ave ☎ 832-2000

Van Cleef & Arpels, 7.
744 Fifth Ave ☎ 644-9500

Victoria's Secret, 16. 34 E 57th St
☎ 758-5592

Warner Bros Studio Store, 9.
1 E 57th St ☎ 754-0300

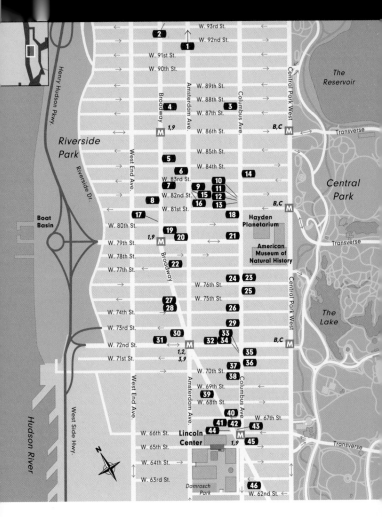

Listed Alphabetically

Madison Square Park

W. 23rd St.

W. 22nd St.

W. 21st St.

W. 20th St.

W. 19th St.

W. 18th St.

W. 17th St.

W. 16th St.

W. 15th St.

W. 14th St.

W. 13th St.

W. 12th St.

W. 11th St.

W. 10th St.

W. 9th St.

W. 8th St.

Tenth Ave.

Ninth Ave.

Eighth Ave.

Seventh Ave.

Ave. of the Americas

Fifth Ave.

Broadway

Flatiron Building

Little W. 12th St.

Gansevoort St.

Horatio St.

Jane St.

Abingdon Sq.

Bethune St.

Bank St.

W. 11th St.

Perry St.

Charles St.

W. 10th St.

Greenwich Ave.

Greenwich St.

Waverly Pl.

Milligan Pl.

Patchin Pl.

Gay St.

GREENWICH VILLAGE

Sheridan Sq.

Waverly Pl.

W. Washington Pl.

MacDougal Alley

Washington Mews

Washington Sq. N.

Washington Square Park

Washington Sq. S.

New York University

Christopher St.

Grove St.

Jones St.

Cornelia St.

Bleecker St.

Commerce St.

Bedford St.

Carmine St.

Barrow St.

Morton St.

St. Luke's Pl.

Leroy St.

Downing St.

Sixth Ave.

MacDougal St.

Sullivan St.

LaGuardia Pl.

Minetta La.

Father Demo Sq.

W. Houston St.

West St.

West Side Hwy.

Washington St.

Greenwich St.

Hudson St.

Listed by Site Number

1. Portico Outlet
2. Comme des Garçons
3. City Quilter
4. Barnes & Noble
5. Reminiscence
6. NY Cake & Baking
7. Restoration Hardware
8. EJ Audi
9. Moe Ginsberg
10. Tootsi Plohound
11. Beckenstein's
12. Sam Flax
13. Fish's Eddy
14. Aveda
15. Bed, Bath & Beyond
16. A Different Light
17. La Maison Moderne
18. Williams Sonoma
19. Hold Everything
20. Sacco
21. Chelsea Market
22. Loehmann's
23. Poster America
24. Old Navy
25. Miya Shoji
26. Books of Wonder
27. Daffy's
28. Barnes & Noble
29. ABC Carpet
30. Paragon
31. Rothman's
32. Barnes & Noble
33. Greenmarket
34. City Bakery
35. Kenneth Cole
36. Beads of Paradise
37. Banana Republic Women's
38. J Crew
39. Banana Rep Men's
40. Paul Smith
41. Joan & David
42. Jensen Lewis
43. Central Carpet
44. Virgin Megastore
45. Forbidden Planet
46. Hyde Park Antiques
47. Strand Books
48. Kiehl's
49. Footlight Records
50. NY Central Art Supply

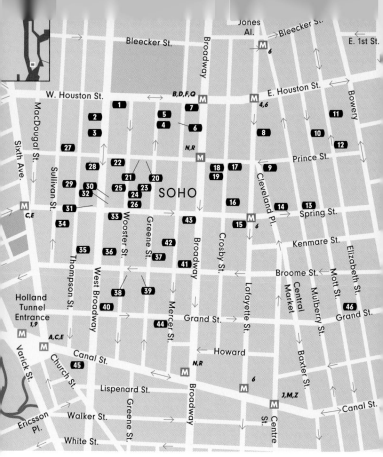

Listed by Site Number

Listed Alphabetically

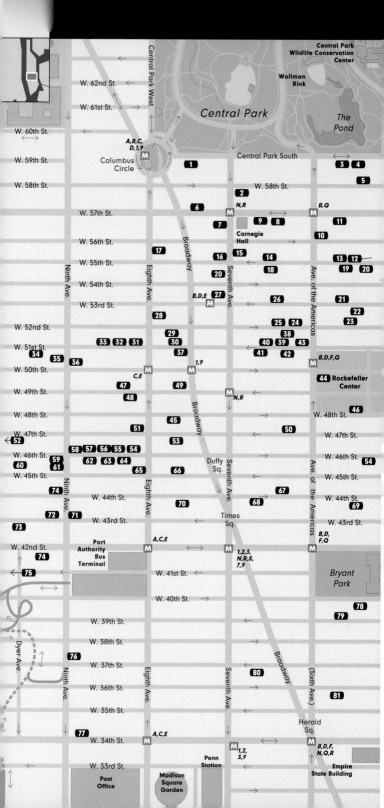

Listed Alphabetically

Adrienne, 90. 700 Fifth Ave
☎ 903–3918. Continental. $$$$

An American Place, 117. 125 E 50th
St ☎ 715–2500. American. $$$

Aquavit, 101. 13 W 54th St
☎ 307–7311. Scandinavian. $$$$

B Smith's, 51. 771 Eighth Ave
☎ 247–2222. Continental. $$$

Bali Nusa Indah, 59. 651 Ninth Ave
☎ 265–2200. Indonesian. $$

Barbetta, 56. 321 W 46th St
☎ 246–9171. Italian. $$$

Becco, 55. 355 W 46th St
☎ 397–7597. Italian. $$

Ben Benson's, 24. 123 W 52nd St
☎ 581–8888. Steakhouse. $$$

Benihana of Tokyo, 91. 120 E 56th St
☎ 593–1627. Japanese. $$

Bienvenue, 136. 21 E 36th St.
☎ 684–0215. French. $$

Billy's, 109. 948 First Ave
☎ 753–1870. American. $$$

Broadway Joe, 54. 315 W 46th St
☎ 246–6513. American. $$

Bryant Park Cafe, 78. 25 W 40th St
☎ 840–6500. American. $$

Bryant Park Grill, 78. 25 W 40th St
☎ 840–6500. American. $$

Café des Sports, 33. 329 W 51st St
☎ 974–9052. French. $$

Café Un Deux Trois, 67. 123 W 44th
St ☎ 354–4148. French. $$

Café St Francis, 73. 482 W 43rd St
☎ 947–6430. American. $$

Caffe Cielo, 28. 881 Eighth Ave
☎ 246–9555. Italian. $$

Captain's Table, 141. 860 Second
Ave ☎ 697–9538. Seafood. $$$

Carnegie Deli, 16. 854 Seventh Ave
☎ 757–2245. Deli. $–$$

Cellini, 96. 65 E 54th St
☎ 751-1555. Italian. $$$

Chez Josephine, 74. 414 W 42nd St
☎ 594–1925. International. $$$

Chez Louis, 44. 74 W 50th St
☎ 333–3388. French. $

Chin Chin, 125. 216 E 49th St
☎ 888–4555. Chinese. $$$

China Grill, 22. 52 W 53rd St
☎ 333–7788. Asian. $$$

Christer's, 14. 145 W 55th St
☎ 974–7224. Scandinavian. $$$

Churrascaria Plataforma, 48.
316 W 49th St ☎ 245–0505. Brazilian. $$

Cité, 44. 120 W 51st St ☎ 956–7100.
Steakhouse. $$$

Colbeh, 79. 43 W 39th St ☎ 334–3181.
Middle Eastern. $–$$

Crepes Suzette, 57. 363 W 46th St
☎ 581–9717. French. $$$

Columbus Bakery, 108. 957 First Ave
☎ 421–0334. Light Fare. $

Dawat, 83. 210 E 58th St ☎ 355–7555.
Indian. $$

Dish of Salt, 50. 133 W 47th St
☎ 921–4242. Cantonese. $$

Dock's on Third, 137. 633 Third Ave
☎ 986–8080. Seafood. $$

Eamonn Doran, 114. 998 Second Ave
☎ 752–8088. Irish. $$

Felidia, 84. 243 E 58th St ☎ 758–1479.
Italian. $$$$

5757, 89. 57 E 57th St ☎ 758-5757.
American. $$$$

Firebird, 58. 365 W 46th St
☎ 586–0244. Russian. $$–$$$

44, 69. 44 W 44th St ☎ 944–8844.
American. $$$

Four Seasons, 112. 99 E 52nd St
☎ 754–9494. American. $$$$

Frankie & Johnny's, 66. 269 W 45th
St ☎ 997–9494. American. $$$

Frico Bar, 71. 402 W 43rd St
☎ 564–7272. Italian. $$

Gallagher's, 29. 228 W 52nd St
☎ 245–5336. Steakhouse. $$$

Grand Central Oyster Bar, 135.
Grand Central Terminal ☎ 490–6650.
Seafood. $$$

Hallo Berlin, 34. 402 W 51st St
☎ 541–6248. German. $

Hard Rock Café, 6. 221 W 57th St
☎ 489–6565. American. $$

Harley Davidson Café, 10.
1370 Sixth Ave ☎ 245–6000.
American. $$

Harry Cipriani, 82. 781 Fifth Ave
☎ 753–5566. Italian. $$$$

Hatsuhana, 131. 17 E 48th St
☎ 355–3345. Japanese. $$$

$$$$ = over $59 $$$ = $40–$59 $$ = $20–$39 $ = under $20
Based on cost per person, excluding drinks, service, and 8¼% sales tax.

Heartbeat, 126. 149 E 49th St
☎ 407-2900. Healthy American.
$$$-$$$$

Heartland Brewery Midtown, 43.
1285 Sixth Ave ☎ 582-8244.
Brewpub. $-$$

Hideaway, 80. 32 W 37th St
☎ 947-8940. Italian. $$$

Houston's, 97. 150 E 53rd St
☎ 888-3828. American. $$

Hurley's, 45. 232 W 48th St
☎ 765-8981. American. $$

Il Nido, 100. 251 E 53rd St
☎ 753-8450. Italian. $$$$

Inagiku, 127. 111 E 49th St
☎ 355-0440. Japanese. $$$

Island Burgers & Shakes, 36.
766 Ninth Ave ☎ 307-7934.
Burgers. $

Joe Allen, 63. 326 W 46th St
☎ 581-6464. American. $$

JUdson Grill, 25. 152 W 52nd St
☎ 582-5252. American. $$$

Keen's, 81. 72 W 36th St
☎ 947-3636. Steakhouse. $$$

Kodama, 65. 301 W 45th St
☎ 582-8065. Japanese. $$

Kuruma Zushi, 132. 7 E 47th St
☎ 317-2802. Japanese. $$$$

La Bonne Soupe, 20. 48 W 55th St
☎ 586-7650. French. $$

La Caravelle, 12. 33 W 55th St
☎ 586-4252. French. $$$$

La Côte Basque, 19. 60 W 55th St
☎ 688-6525. French. $$$$

La Grenouille, 113. 3 E 52nd St
☎ 752-1495. French. $$$$

La Reserve, 130. 4 W 49th St
☎ 247-2993. French. $$$$

Le Bernardin, 40. 155 W 51st St
☎ 489-1515. Seafood. $$$$

Le Cirque 2000, 113. 455 Madison
Ave ☎ 303-7788. French. $$$$

Le Colonial, 88. 149 E 57th St
☎ 752-0808. Vietnamese. $$

Le Madeleine, 72. 403 W 43rd St
☎ 246-2993. French. $$

L'Entrecote, 87. 1057 First Ave
☎ 755-0080. French. $$$

Le Perigord, 110. 405 E 52nd St
☎ 755-6244. French. $$$$

Le Rivage, 62. 340 W 46th St
☎ 765-7374. French. $$

Les Pyrénées, 30. 251 W 51st St
☎ 246-0044. French. $$$

Lespinasse, 94. 2 E 55th St
☎ 339-6719. French. $$$$

Lipstick Café, 99. 885 Third Ave
☎ 486-8664. Continental. $$

Lutèce, 120. 249 E 50th St
☎ 752-2225. French. $$$$

Maloney & Porcelli, 116. 37 E 50th St
☎ 750-2233. American. $$-$$$

Mangia, 11. 50 W 57th St
☎ 582-3061. Italian. $

Manhattan Ocean Club, 5. 57 W
58th St ☎ 371-7777. Seafood. $$$

Maple Garden Duckhouse, 106. 236
E 53rd St ☎ 759-8260. Chinese. $-$$

March, 85. 405 E 58th St ☎ 754-6272.
Eclectic. $$$$

Marichu, 140. 342 E 46th St
☎ 370-1866. Basque. $$$

Market Café, 76. 357 Ninth Ave
☎ 967-3892. American. $$

Mars 2112, 37. 1633 Broadway
☎ 582-2112. Eclectic. $$

Meskerem, 52. 468 W 47th St
☎ 664-0520. Ethiopian. $

**Michael Jordan's The Steak House
NYC, 134.** 23 Vanderbilt Ave
☎ 635-2300. Steakhouse. $$$

Mickey Mantle's, 3. 42 Central
Park S ☎ 688-7777. American. $$

Mike's American Bar and Grill, 60.
650 Tenth Ave ☎ 246-4115. American. $$

Molyvos, 15. 871 Seventh Ave
☎ 582-7500. Greek. $$-$$$

Morton's of Chicago, 133. 551 Fifth
Ave ☎ 972-3315. Steakhouse. $$$$

Nanni, 138. 146 E 46th St ☎ 697-4161.
Italian. $$$$

New World Grill, 47. 329 W 49th St
☎ 957-4757. Eclectic. $$

Nippon, 111. 155 E 52nd St
☎ 355-9020. Japanese. $$$

Nirvana, 4. 30 Central Park S
☎ 486-5700. Indian. $$$

Oceana, 95. 55 E 54th St
☎ 759-5941. Seafood. $$$$

Orso, 64. 322 W 46th St ☎ 489-7212.
Italian. $$$

Osteria del Circo, 18. 120 W 55th St
☎ 265-3636. Italian. $$$

Palio, 39. 151 W 51st St ☎ 245-4850.
Italian. $$$$

Palm, 143. 837 Second Ave
☎ 687-2953. Steakhouse. $$$

Patroon, 139. 160 E 46th St
☎ 883-7373. American. $$$

Peacock Alley, 128. 301 Park Ave
☎ 872-4895. French. $$$$

Petrossian, 2. 182 W 58th St
☎ 245-2214. Continental. $$$$

Pierre au Tunnel, 53. 250 W 47th St
☎ 575-1220. French. $$

PJ Clarke's, 93. 915 Third Ave
☎ 759-1650. American. $

Planet Hollywood, 8. 140 W 57th St
☎ 333-7827. American. $$

Raphael, 21. 33 W 54th St
☎ 582-8993. French. $$$$

Remi, 26. 145 W 53rd St ☎ 581-4242.
Italian. $$$

René Pujol, 32. 321 W 51st St
☎ 246-3023. French. $$$

Rosa Mexicano, 86. 1063 First Ave
☎ 753-7407. Mexican. $$

Russian Tea Room, 9. 150 W 57th St
☎ 974-2111. Russian. $$$$

Ruth's Chris Steakhouse, 41. 148 W
51st St ☎ 245-9600. Steakhouse. $$$

San Domenico, 1. 240 Central Park S
☎ 265-5959. Italian. $$$$

San Giusto, 123. 935 Second Ave
☎ 319-0900. Italian. $$$

San Pietro, 102. 18 E 54th St
☎ 753-9015. Italian. $$$

Sardi's, 70. 234 W 44th St
☎ 221-8444. Continental. $$$

Scarabée, 119. 230 E 51st St
☎ 758-6633. Mediterranean. $$-$$$

Seryna, 104. 11 E 53rd St
☎ 980-9393. Japanese. $$$$

Shaan, 46. Rockefeller Ctr,
57 W 48th St ☎ 977-8400. Indian. $$

Shun Lee Palace, 92. 155 E 55th St
☎ 371-8844. Chinese. $$$

Sichuan Palace, 144. 310 E 44th St
☎ 972-7377. Chinese. $$

Smith & Wollensky, 124. 797 Third
Ave ☎ 753-1530. Steakhouse. $$$

Solera, 105. 216 E 53rd St
☎ 644-1166. Spanish. $$

Soul Fixins', 77. 371 W 34th St
☎ 736-1345. Soul. $

Spark's Steak House, 142.
210 E 46th St ☎ 687-4855.
Steakhouse. $$$

Stage Deli, 27. 834 Seventh Ave
☎ 245-7850. Deli. $

Sushiden, 129. 19 E 49th St
☎ 758-2700. Japanese. $$$

Sushisay, 114. 38 E 51st St
☎ 755-1780. Japanese. $$$

Tang Pavilion, 13. 65 W 55th St
☎ 956-6888. Chinese. $$-$$$

Tapika, 17. 950 Eighth Ave
☎ 397-3737. Southwestern. $$-$$$

Tatou, 118. 151 E 50th St ☎ 753-1144.
New American. $$$

Tea Box, 103. Takashimaya, 693 Fifth
Ave ☎ 350-0100. Eclectic. $$

Tout Va Bien, 31. 311 W 51st St
☎ 265-0190. French. $$

Trattoria dell'Arte, 7. 900 Seventh
Ave ☎ 245-9800. Italian. $$$.

Tse Yang, 115. 34 E 51st St
☎ 688-5447. Chinese. $$$-$$$$

21 Club, 23. 21 W 52nd St
☎ 582-7200. American. $$$$

Uncle Nick's, 35. 747 Ninth Ave
☎ 245-7992. Greek. $-$$

Via Brasil, 54. 34 W 46th St
☎ 997-1158. Brazilian. $$

Victor's Café, 38. 236 W 52nd St
☎ 586-7714. Cuban. $$-$$$

Virgil's Real BBQ, 68. 152 W 44th St
☎ 921-9494. Barbecue. $

Vong, 98. 200 E 54th St ☎ 486-9592.
Thai Fusion. $$$

Wally's & Joseph's, 49. 249 W 49th St
☎ 582-0460. Steakhouse. $$$

World Yacht Cruises, 75. Pier 81, W
41st St ☎ 630-8100. Continental. $$$$

Wylie's Ribs & Co, 122. 891 First Ave
☎ 751-0700. Barbecue. $$

Zarela, 121. 953 Second Ave
☎ 644-6740. Mexican. $$

Zen Palate, 61. 663 Ninth Ave
☎ 582-1669. Vegetarian. $$

$$$$ = over $60 $$$ = $40-$59 $$ = $20-$39 $ = under $20
Based on cost per person, excluding drinks, service, and 8⅛% sales tax.

MAP **50** **Restaurants/Upper West Side**

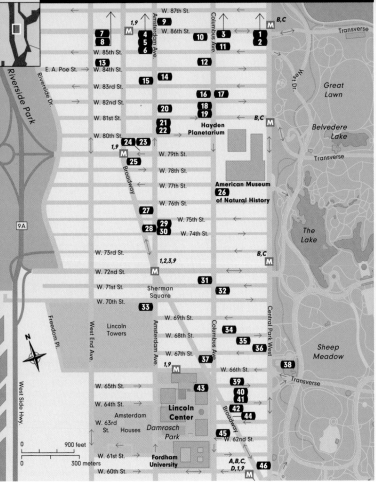

Listed by Site Number

1 Charlie's	17 Fujiyama Mama	33 Café Luxembourg
2 Sylvia's	18 Rain	34 La Boîte en Bois
3 Terrace	19 Main Street	35 Vince & Eddie's
4 Pampa	20 EJ's Luncheonette	36 Café des Artistes
5 Gabriela's	21 Haru	37 Ollie's
6 Gennaro	22 Sarabeth's Kitchen	38 Tavern on the Green
7 Dock's Oyster Bar & Grill	23 Savann	39 Shun Lee West
8 Carmine's	24 Two Two Two	40 John's Pizzeria
9 Barney Greengrass	25 Ruby Foo's Dim Sum Palace	41 O'Neal's
10 La Mirabelle	26 Isabella's	42 Picholine
11 Delphini	27 Ernie's	43 Panevino
12 Avenue	28 Josie's	44 Cafe Fiorello
13 Edgar's Cafe	29 Gabriela's	44 Josephina
14 Good Enough to Eat	30 Shark Bar	45 Merlot Bar & Grill
15 Fred's	31 Penang	46 Jean Georges
16 Columbus Bakery	32 Pasha	

Listed Alphabetically

Avenue, 12. 520 Columbus Ave
☎ 579-3194. French. $$

Barney Greengrass, 9.
541 Amsterdam Ave ☎ 724-4707.
Deli. $$

Café des Artistes, 36. 1 W 67th St
☎ 877-3500. French. $$$$

Cafe Fiorello, 44. 1900 Broadway
☎ 595-5330. Italian. $$

Café Luxembourg, 33. 200 W 70th St
☎ 873-7411. American. $$$

Calle Ocho, 19. 446 Columbus Ave
☎ 873-5025. Pan-Latin. $$

Carmine's, 8. 2450 Broadway
☎ 362-2200. Italian. $$

Charlie's Southern Style Chicken, 1.
2839 Eighth Ave ☎ 926-4313. Soul. $

Columbus Bakery, 16. 474 Columbus
Ave ☎ 724-6880. Light Fare. $

Delphini, 11. 519 Columbus Ave
☎ 579-1145. Mediterranean. $$

Dock's Oyster Bar & Grill, 7. 2427
B'way ☎ 724-5588. Seafood. $$

EJ's Luncheonette, 20.
447 Amsterdam Ave ☎ 873-3444.
American. $

Edgar's Cafe, 13. 255 W 84th St
☎ 496-6126. Dessert. $

Ernie's, 27. 2150 Broadway
☎ 496-1588. Italian. $$

Fred's, 15. 476 Amsterdam Ave
☎ 579-3076. American. $-$$

Fujiyama Mama, 17. 467 Columbus
Ave ☎ 769-1144. Japanese. $$

Gabriela's, 5. 685 Amsterdam Ave
☎ 961-0574. Mexican. $

Gabriela's, 29. 311 Amsterdam Ave
☎ 875-8532. Mexican. $

Gennaro, 6. 665 Amsterdam Ave
☎ 665-5348. Italian. $$

Good Enough to Eat, 14. 483
Amsterdam Ave ☎ 496-0163.
American. $$

Haru, 21. 433 Amsterdam Ave
☎ 579-5655. Japanese. $$

Isabella's, 26. 359 Columbus Ave
☎ 724-2100. Mediterranean. $$

Jean Georges, 46. 1 Central Park W
☎ 299-3900. French. $$$$

John's Pizzeria, 40. 48 W 65th St
☎ 721-7001. Italian. $

Josephina, 44. 1900 Broadway
☎ 799-1000. American. $$

Josie's, 28. 300 Amsterdam Ave
☎ 769-1212. American. $$

La Boîte en Bois, 34. 75 W 68th
St ☎ 874-2705. French. $$

La Mirabelle, 10. 102 W 86th St
☎ 496-0458. French. $$

Merlot Bar & Grill, 45. 48 W 63rd St
☎ 363-7568. French/American. $$

Ollie's, 37. 1991 Broadway
☎ 595-8181. Chinese. $

O'Neal's, 41. 49 W 64th St
☎ 787-4663. American. $$

Pampa, 4. 768 Amsterdam Ave
☎ 865-2929. Steakhouse. $$

Panevino, 43. Lincoln Center,
Broadway & W 65th St ☎ 874-7000.
Continental. $$

Pasha, 32. 70 W 71st St ☎ 579-8751.
Turkish. $$

Penang, 31. 240 Columbus Ave
☎ 769-3988. Malaysian. $

Picholine, 42. 35 W 64th St
☎ 724-8585. French. $$$$

Rain, 18. 100 W 82nd St
☎ 501-0776. Pan-Asian. $$

Ruby Foo's Dim Sum Palace, 25.
2182 Broadway ☎ 724-6700.
Chinese. $$

Sarabeth's Kitchen, 22.
423 Amsterdam Ave
☎ 496-6280. American. $$

Savann, 23. 414 Amsterdam Ave
☎ 580-0202. French. $$

Shark Bar, 30. 307 Amsterdam Ave
☎ 874-8500. Southern. $$

Shun Lee West, 39. 43 W 65th St
☎ 595-8895. Chinese. $$$

Sylvia's, 2. 328 Lenox Ave
☎ 996-0660. Soul. $$

Tavern on the Green, 38. Central
Park W & 67th St ☎ 873-3200.
Continental. $$$

Terrace, 3. 400 W 119th St
☎ 666-9490. French. $$$

Two Two Two, 24. 222 W 79th St
☎ 799-0400. New American. $$$

Vince & Eddie's, 36. 70 W 68th St
☎ 721-0068. American. $$$

Aureole, 41. 34 E 61st St ☎ 319-1660. New American. $$$$

Bolivar, 46. 206 E 60th St ☎ 838-0440. Pan-Latin. $$-$$$

Bravo Gianni, 37. 230 E 63rd St ☎ 752-7272. Italian. $$$

Café Boulud, 20. 20 E 76th St ☎ 772-2600. French. $$$$

Café Crocodile, 27. 354 E 74th St ☎ 249-6619. Mediterranean. $$$

Canyon Road, 24. 1470 First Ave ☎ 734-1600. Southwestern. $$$

Carlyle Restaurant, 19. Carlyle Hotel, 35 E 76th St ☎ 744-1600. French. $$$$

Comfort Diner, 4. 142 E 86th St ☎ 369-8628. American. $

Daniel, 33. 60 E 65th St ☎ 288-0033. French. $$$$

Destinée, 43. 134 E 61st St ☎ 888-1220. French. $$$-$$$$

EAT, 15. 1064 Madison Ave ☎ 772-0022. American. $$$

El Pollo, 2. 1746 First Ave ☎ 996-7810. Peruvian. $

Etats-Unis, 11. 242 E 81st St ☎ 517-8826. Eclectic. $$

First Wok, 17. 1374 Third Ave ☎ 861-2600. Chinese. $

Heidelberg, 5. 1648 Second Ave ☎ 628-2332. German. $$

JG Melon, 28. 1291 Third Ave ☎ 744-0585. American. $$

Jo Jo, 35. 160 E 64th St ☎ 223-5656. French. $$$

Le Regence, 34. 37 E 64th St ☎ 606-4647. French. $$$$

The Lobster Club, 14. 24 E 80th St ☎ 249-6500. American. $$$

Lusardi's, 22. 1494 Second Ave ☎ 249-2020. Italian. $$$$

Madame Romaine, 42. 132 E 61st St ☎ 758-2422. French. $$

Mark's Restaurant, 18. 25 E 77th St ☎ 879-1864. Continental. $$$

Matthew's, 44. 1030 Third Ave ☎ 838-4343. Mediterranean. $$$

Maxim's, 39. 680 Madison Ave ☎ 751-5111. French. $$$$

Maya, 36. 1191 First Ave ☎ 585-1818. Mexican. $$$

Mezzaluna, 29. 1295 Third Ave ☎ 535-9600. Italian. $$$

Mocca, 8. 1588 Second Ave ☎ 734-6470. Hungarian. $$

Pamir, 25. 1437 Second Ave ☎ 650-1095. Afghan. $$

Parioli Romanissimo, 13. 24 E 81st St ☎ 288-2391. Italian. $$$$

Park Avenue Café, 40. 100 E 63rd St ☎ 644-1900. American. $$$$

Payard Pâtisserie & Bistro, 30. 1032 Lexington Ave ☎ 717-5252. French. $$-$$$$

Persepolis, 26. 1423 Second Ave ☎ 535-1100. Persian. $$

Petaluma, 31. 1356 First Ave ☎ 772-8800. Italian. $$$

Pig Heaven, 9. 1540 Second Ave ☎ 744-4333. Chinese. $$

Post House, 38. 28 E 63rd St ☎ 935-2888. American. $$$$

Right Bank, 32. 822 Madison Ave ☎ 737-2811. American. $$

Sarabeth's at the Whitney, 21. 1295 Madison Ave ☎ 570-3670. American. $

Serendipity 3, 45. 225 E 60th St ☎ 838-3531. American. $$

Sistina, 10. 1555 Second Ave ☎ 861-7660. Italian. $$$

Table d'Hote, 1. 44 E 92nd St ☎ 348-8125. French. $$$

Trois Jean, 16. 154 E 79th St ☎ 988-4858. French. $$$

Vermicelli, 23. 1492 Second Ave ☎ 288-8868. Vietnamese. $

Vespa Cibobuono, 6. 1625 Second Ave ☎ 472-2050. Italian. $$

Wilkinson's, 7. 1573 York Ave ☎ 535-5454. Seafood. $$$

Wu Liang Ye, 3. 215 E 86th St ☎ 534-8899. Chinese. $

Zócalo, 12. 174 E 82nd St ☎ 717-7772. Mexican. $$-$$$

$$$$ = over $60 $$$ = $40-$59 $$ = $20-$39 $ = under $20
Based on cost per person, excluding drinks, service, and 8 ¼% sales tax.

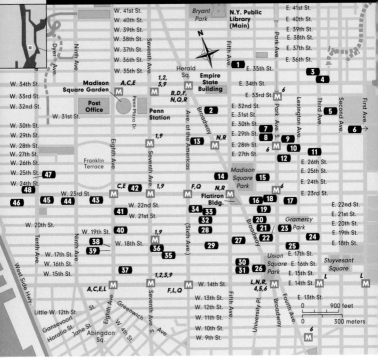

$$$$ = *over $50* $$$ = *$30-$50* $$ = *$20-$30* $ = *under $20*
Based on cost per person, excluding drinks, service, and 8 1/4% sales tax.

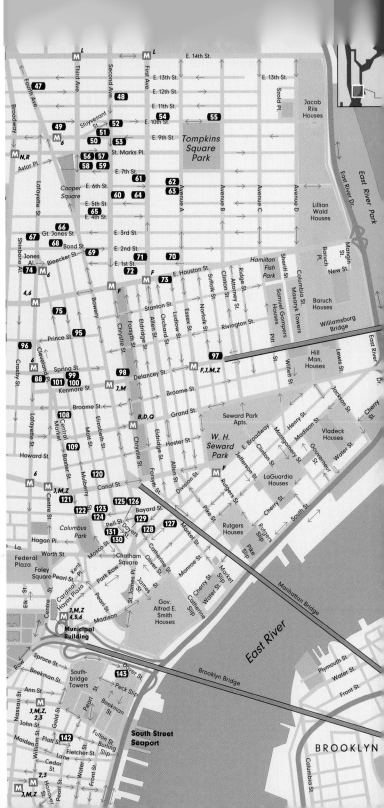

Listed by Site Number

Acme Bar & Grill, 67. 9 Great Jones St ☎ 420-1934. Southern. $

Aggie's, 45. 146 W Houston St ☎ 673-8994. American. $

Alison on Dominick Street, 103. 38 Dominick St ☎ 727-1188. French. $$$

American Park at the Battery, 141. Battery Pk, opposite 175 State St ☎ 809-5508. American. $$$

Angelica Kitchen, 48. 300 E 12th St ☎ 228-2909. Vegetarian. $

Angelo's, 109. 146 Mulberry St ☎ 966-1277. Italian. $$

Aquagrill, 85. 210 Spring St. ☎ 274-0505. Seafood. $$$

Arqua, 136. 281 Church St ☎ 334-1888. Italian. $$$

Arturo's, 46. 106 Houston St ☎ 677-3820. Pizza. $

Babbo, 15. 110 Waverly Pl ☎ 777-0303. Italian. $$$-$$$$

Balthazar, 93. 80 Spring St ☎ 965-1414. French. $$$

Bar Pitti, 41. 268 Sixth Ave ☎ 982-3300. Italian. $$

Barocco, 110. 301 Church St ☎ 431-1445. Italian. $$

Benito II, 108. 163 Mulberry St ☎ 226-9012. Italian. $$

Benny's Burritos, 3. 113 Greenwich Ave ☎ 727-0584. Mexican. $

Blue Ribbon, 83. 97 Sullivan St ☎ 274-0404. Eclectic. $$-$$$

Blue Ribbon Bakery, 43. 33 Downing St ☎ 337-0404. French. $$

Blue Ribbon Sushi, 94. 119 Sullivan St ☎ 343-0404. Japanese. $$-$$$

Bo-Ky, 124. 80 Bayard St ☎ 406-2292. Vietnamese. $

Boca Chica, 71. 13 First Ave ☎ 473-0108. Latin. $$

Bop, 69. 325 Bowery ☎ 254-7887. Korean. $$

Bouley Bakery, 137. 120 W Broadway ☎ 964-2525. French. $$$-$$$$

Bridge Cafe, 143. 279 Water St ☎ 227-3344. American. $$

Brothers Bar-B-Q, 44. 225 Varick St ☎ 727-2775. Barbecue. $

Bubby's, 115. 120 Hudson St ☎ 219-0666. American. $-$$

Café de Bruxelles, 2. 118 Greenwich Ave ☎ 206-1830. Belgian. $$

Cafe Habana, 95. 17 Prince St ☎ 625-2001. Cuban. $

Café Loup, 5. 105 W 13th St ☎ 255-4746. French. $$

Café Milou, 21. 92 Seventh Ave ☎ 414-9824. French. $-$$

Cafe Spice, 9. 72 University Pl ☎ 253-6999. Indian. $$

Campo, 4. 89 Greenwich Ave ☎ 691-8080. Pan-Latin. $$

Canton, 128. 45 Division St ☎ 226-4441. Chinese. $$

Capsouto Frères, 104. 451 Washington St ☎ 966-4900. French. $$$

Caribe, 17. 117 Perry St ☎ 255-9191. Jamaican. $$

Cendrillon, 102. 45 Mercer St ☎ 343-9012. Philippine. $$

Cent' Anni, 32. 50 Carmine St ☎ 989-9494. Italian. $$$

Chanterelle, 119. 2 Harrison St ☎ 966-6960. French. $$$$

Chez Jacqueline, 38. 72 McDougal St ☎ 505-0727. $$$

Chez es Saada, 72. 42 E First St ☎ 777-5617. Moroccan. $$

City Hall, 135. 131 Duane St ☎ 227-7777. American. $$-$$$

Clementine, 14. 1 Fifth Ave. ☎ 253-0003. American. $$$

Cucina di Pesce, 65. 87 E 4th St ☎ 260-6800. Italian. $-$$

Cucina Stagionale, 27. 275 Bleecker St ☎ 924-2707. Italian. $

Danal, 49. 90 E Tenth St ☎ 982-6930. French. $-$$

Dojo, 56. 24 St Marks Pl ☎ 674-9821. Vegetarian. $

Drovers Tap Room, 23. 9 Jones St ☎ 627-1233. American. $$

Duane Park Café, 133. 157 Duane St ☎ 732-5555. American. $$$

Eastern Villa, 123. 66 Mott St ☎ 226-4675. Chinese. $$

$$$$ = over $60 $$$ = $40-$59 $$ = $20-$39 $ = under $20
Based on cost per person, excluding drinks, service, and 8¼% sales tax.

Listed Alphabetically (cont.)

Ecco, 138. 124 Chambers St
☎ 227-7074. Italian. $$$

El Teddy's, 112. 219 W
Broadway ☎ 941-7070.
Mexican. $$

Elephant & Castle, 10. 68 Greenwich
Ave ☎ 243-1400. American. $$

Ennio & Michael, 36. 539 LaGuardia
Pl ☎ 677-8577. Italian. $$

EQ Restaurant, 12. 267 Fourth St
☎ 414-1961. French. $$$

Fanelli, 90. 94 Prince St
☎ 226-9412. American. $

Felix, 106. 340 W Broadway
☎ 431-0021. French. $$

Florent, 1. 69 Gansevoort St
☎ 989-5779. French. $$

First, 64. 87 First Ave ☎ 674-3123.
American. $$

Fraunces Tavern, 142. 54 Pearl St
☎ 269-0144. American. $$

French Roast, 6. 458 Sixth Ave
☎ 533-2233. French. $

Frontière, 78. 199 Prince St.
☎ 387-0898. French/Italian. $$$

Ghenet, 75. 284 Mulberry St
☎ 343-1888. Ethiopian. $

Gotham Bar & Grill, 8. 12 E 12th St
☎ 620-4020. American. $$$$

Grange Hall, 30. 50 Commercial St
☎ 924-5246. American. $-$$

Great Jones Café, 66. 54 Great
Jones St ☎ 674-9304. American. $

Haveli, 60. 100 Second Ave
☎ 982-0533. Indian. $$

Holy Basil, 51. 149 Second Ave
☎ 460-5557. Thai. $-$$

Home, 25. 20 Cornelia St
☎ 243-9579. American. $$

Honmura An, 92. 170 Mercer St
☎ 334-5253. Japanese. $$$

Hudson River Club, 139.
4 World Financial Ctr ☎ 786-1500.
American. $$$$

Il Buco, 68. 47 Bond St
☎ 533-1932. Italian. $$-$$$

Il Mulino, 35. 86 W 3rd St
☎ 673-3783. Italian. $$$

The Independent, 114. 179 W B'way
☎ 219-2110. American. $$$

Indigo, 13. 142 W 10th St
☎ 691-7757. American/Eclectic. $$

Japonica, 7. 100 University Pl
☎ 243-7752. Japanese. $$

Jean Claude, 79. 137 Sullivan St
☎ 475-9232. French. $$

Jing Fong, 125. 20 Elizabeth St
☎ 964-5256. Chinese. $-$$

Joe's Shanghai, 126. 9 Pell St.
☎ 233-8888. Chinese. $

John's Pizzeria, 28. 278 Bleecker St
☎ 243-1680. Pizza. $

Katz's Delicatessen, 73. 205 E
Houston St ☎ 254-2246. Deli. $

Khyber Pass, 57. 34 St Mark's Pl
☎ 473-0989. Afghan. $$

La Boheme, 33. 24 Minetta La
☎ 473-6447. French. $$

La Metairie, 16. 189 W 10th St
☎ 989-0343. French. $$-$$$$

La Paella, 50. 214 E Ninth St
☎ 598-4321. Spanish. $$

Layla, 113. 211 W Broadway
☎ 431-0700. Middle Eastern. $$$

Le Figaro, 37. 184 Bleecker St
☎ 677-1100. American. $

Le Jardin Bistro, 101. 25 Cleveland Pl
☎ 343-9599. French. $-$$

Le Pescadou, 76. 16 King St
☎ 924-3434. French. $$$

Life Cafe, 55. 343 E 10th St
☎ 477-8791. Vegetarian. $

Lombardi's, 99. 32 Spring St
☎ 941-7994. Pizza. $

Lucky Strike, 107. 59 Grand St
☎ 941-0479. French/American. $$

Mekka, 70. 14 Avenue A.
☎ 475-8500. Soul Food. $$

Mercer Kitchen, 89. 99 Prince St
☎ 966-5454. French. $$-$$$

Mezzogiorno, 84. 195 Spring St
☎ 334-2112. Italian. $$

Miracle Grill, 61. 112 First Ave
☎ 254-2353. Southwestern. $$

Montrachet, 111. 239 W Broadway
☎ 219-2777. French. $$$-$$$$

Moustache, 29. 90 Bedford St
☎ 229-2220. Middle Eastern. $

Moustache, 54. 265 E Tenth St
☎ 228-2022. Middle Eastern. $

Nha Trang, 121. 87 Baxter St
☎ 233-5948. Vietnamese. $

Nice, 127. 35 E Broadway
☎ 406-9510. Chinese. $$

Nobu, 116. 105 Hudson St
☎ 219-0500. Japanese. $$$$

NoHo Star, 74. 330 Lafayette St
☎ 925-0070. American. $-$$

Odeon, 132. 145 W Broadway
☎ 233-0507. American. $$

Omen, 82. 113 Thompson St
☎ 925-8923. Japanese. $$$

One If By Land, Two If By Sea, 22.
17 Barrow St ☎ 228-0822.
Continental. $$$

Opaline, 63. 85 Avenue A
☎ 475-5050. American. $$

Pearl Oyster Bar, 26. 18 Cornelia St
☎ 691-8211. Seafood. $$

Peking Duck House, 131. 22 Mott St
☎ 227-1810. Chinese. $$

Petite Abeille, 31. 466 Hudson St
☎ 741-6479. Belgian. $

Pink Tea Cup, 19. 42 Grove St
☎ 807-6755. Soul. $

Pisces, 62. 95 Avenue A
☎ 260-6660. Seafood. $$

Pó, 24. 31 Cornelia St ☎ 645-2189.
Italian. $$

Pommes Frites, 59. 123 Second Ave.
☎ 674-1234. Belgian. $

Pop, 47. 127 Fourth Ave
☎ 674-8713. Eclectic. $$$

Provence, 77. 38 MacDougal St
☎ 475-7500. French. $$$

Quantum Leap, 34. 88 W 3rd St
☎ 677-8050. Vegetarian. $$

Quilty's, 80. 177 Prince St
☎ 254-1260. New American. $$-$$$

Raoul's, 81. 180 Prince St
☎ 966-3518. French. $$$

Ratner's, 97. 138 Delancey St
☎ 677-5588. Kosher. $

Restaurant Boughalem, 42. 14
Bedford St ☎ 414-4764. Belgian. $$

Rice, 100. 227 Mott St ☎ 226-5775.
Eclectic. $

Salaam Bombay, 134. 317
Greenwich St ☎ 226-9400. Indian. $$

Sammy's Roumanian, 98.
157 Chrystie St ☎ 673-0030.
Eastern European. $$$

Savoy, 96. 70 Prince St. ☎ 219-8570.
Mediterranean/American. $$$

Sazerac House Bar & Grill, 18.
533 Hudson St ☎ 989-0313.
Cajun. $$

Second Ave Deli, 52. 156
Second Ave ☎ 677-0606. Deli. $-$$

Soho Kitchen, 87. 103 Greene St
☎ 925-1866. American. $$

Spartina, 118. 355 Greenwich
St ☎ 274-9310. Mediterranean.
$$-$$$

Spring Street Natural, 88. 62 Spring
St ☎ 966-0290. Vegetarian. $$

Surya, 20. 302 Bleecker St
☎ 807-7777. Indian. $$

Tennessee Mountain, 86. 143 Spring
St ☎ 431-3993. Barbecue. $$

Thailand, 122. 106 Bayard St
☎ 349-3132. Thai. $

Tomoe Sushi, 39. 172 Thompson St
☎ 777-9346. Japanese. $$

Tribeca Grill, 117. 375 Greenwich St
☎ 941-3900. Seafood. $$$

Triplet's Roumanian, 105. 11-17
Grand St ☎ 925-9303. East
European. $$$

20 Mott St, 130. 20 Mott St
☎ 964-0380. Chinese. $$

Veselka, 53. 144 Second Ave
☎ 228-9682. East European. $

Viet-Nam, 129. 11-13 Doyers St
☎ 693-0725. Vietnamese. $

Villa Mosconi, 40. 69 MacDougal St
☎ 673-0390. Italian. $$

Windows on the World, 140.
1 World Trade Center, 107th Floor.
☎ 524-7000. American. $$$$

Wong Kee, 120. 113 Mott St
☎ 966-1160. Chinese. $

Ye Waverly Inn, 11. 16 Bank St
☎ 929-4377. American. $$

Zoë, 91. 90 Prince St
☎ 966-6722. American. $$$

$$$$ = over $60 $$$ = $40-$59 $$ = $20-$39 $ = under $20
Based on cost per person, excluding drinks, service, and 8¼% sales tax.

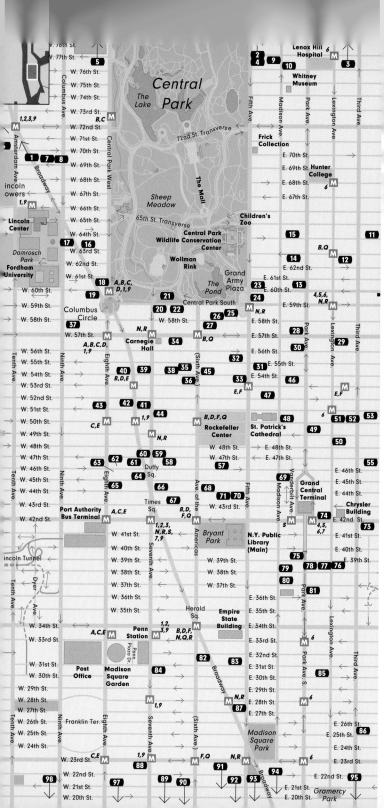

Listed Alphabetically (cont.)

Millennium Broadway, 66. 145 W 44th St ☎ 768-4400. 📠 768-0847. $$

Morgans, 80. 237 Madison Ave ☎ 686-0300. 📠 779-8352. $$$

NY Helmsley, 73. 212 E 42nd St ☎ 490-8900. 📠 986-4792. $$

NY Hilton, 45. 1335 Sixth Ave ☎ 586-7000. 📠 261-5902. $$$

NY Palace, 51. 455 Madison Ave ☎ 888-7000. 📠 303-6000. $$$

NY Marriott WTC, 98. 3 World Trade Ctr ☎ 938-9100. 📠 321-2107. $$$$

Novotel, 42. 226 W 52nd St ☎ 315-0100. 📠 765-5365. $$

Omni Berkshire Place, 47. 21 E 52nd St ☎ 753-5800. 📠 754-5020. $$$$

Paramount, 62. 235 W 46th St ☎ 764-5500. 📠 575-4892. $$-$$$

The Peninsula, 33. 700 Fifth Ave ☎ 247-2200. 📠 903-3943. $$$$

Pickwick Arms, 53. 230 E 51st St ☎ 355-0300. 📠 755-5945. $

Pierre, 23. 2 E 61st St ☎ 838-8000. 📠 758-1615. $$$$

The Plaza, 25. Fifth Ave & 59th St ☎ 759-3000. 📠 546-5324. $$$$

Plaza Athénée, 15. 37 E 64th St ☎ 734-9100. 📠 772-0958. $$$$

Plaza Fifty, 51. 155 E 50th St ☎ 751-5710. 📠 753-1468. $$$

Portland Square Hotel, 58. 132 W 47th St ☎ 382-0600. 📠 382-0684. $

Quality Hotel East Side, 85. 161 Lexington Ave ☎ 532-2255. 📠 790-2758. $$

Quality Hotel and Suites, 57. 59 W 46th St ☎ 719-2300. $$

Radisson Empire, 17. 44 W 63rd St ☎ 265-7400. 📠 244-3382. $$

Ramada Milford Plaza, 65. 270 W 45 St ☎ 869-3600 📠 642-4694. $$

Regal UN Plaza, 56. 1 UN Plaza ☎ 758-1234. 📠 702-5051. $$$$

Regency, 13. 540 Park Ave ☎ 759-4100. 📠 826-5674. $$$$

Renaissance, 59. 714 7th Ave ☎ 765-7676. 📠 765-1962. $$$

Rihga Royal, 38. 151 W 54th St ☎ 307-5000. 📠 765-6530. $$$$

Roger Smith, 50. 501 Lexington Ave ☎ 755-1400. 📠 758-4061. $$

Roosevelt, 69. 45 E 45th St ☎ 661-9600. 📠 885-6161. $$

Royalton, 71. 44 W 44th St ☎ 869-4400. 📠 575-0012. $$$

St Regis, 31. 2 E 55th St ☎ 753-4500. 📠 787-3447. $$$$

San Carlos, 52. 150 E 50th St ☎ 755-1800. 📠 688-9778. $$

Sheraton Manhattan, 41. 790 Seventh Ave ☎ 581-3300. 📠 621-8920. $$

Sheraton Russell, 81. 45 Park Ave ☎ 685-7676. 📠 889-3193. $$-$$$

Sherry Netherland, 24. 781 Fifth Ave ☎ 355-2800. 📠 319-4306. $$$$

Shoreham, 32. 33 W 55th St ☎ 247-6700. 📠 765-9741. $$$-$$$$

SoHo Grand, 97. 310 W Broadway ☎ 965-3000 📠 965-3244. $$$

Southgate Tower, 84. 371 Seventh Ave ☎ 563-1800. 📠 643-8028. $$

Stanhope, 4. 995 Fifth Ave ☎ 288-5800. 📠 650-4705. $$$

Trump International Hotel & Towers, 19. 1 Central Park West ☎ 299-1000. 📠 299-1150. $$$-$$$$

Vanderbilt YMCA, 55. 224 E 47th St ☎ 756-9600. 📠 752-0210. $

W New York—The Court, 76. 130 E 39th St ☎ 685-1100. 📠 889-0287. $$$

W New York—Tuscany, 77. 120 E 39th St ☎ 779-7822. 📠 696-2095. $$$

Waldorf-Astoria, 49. 301 Park Ave ☎ 355-3000. 📠 872-7272. $$$$

Warwick, 45. 65 W 54th St ☎ 247-2700. 📠 489-3926. $$$

Washington Square, 92. 103 Waverly Pl ☎ 777-9515. 📠 979-8373. $

Wellington, 39. 871 Seventh Ave ☎ 247-3900. 📠 581-1719. $$

West Side YMCA, 16. 5 W 63rd St ☎ 787-4400. 📠 875-1334. $

Westin Central Park South, 21. 112 Central Park S ☎ 757-1900. 📠 757-9620. $$$

Westpark Hotel, 37. 308 W 58th St ☎ 246-6440. 📠 246-3131. $

$$$$ = over $400 $$$ = $275-$400 $$ = $150-$275 $ = under $150
All prices are for a standard double room, excluding 13¼% city and state sales tax and $2 occupancy tax.

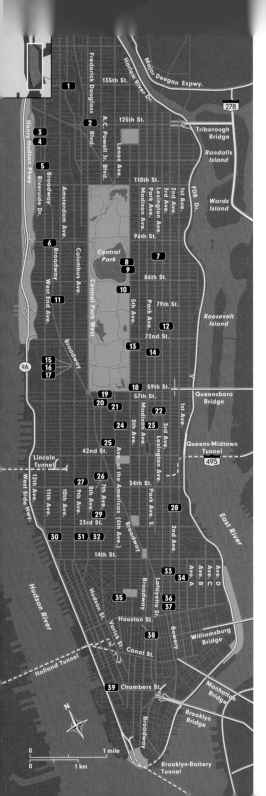

Listed Alphabetically

Aaron Davis Hall, 1. 135 Convent Ave ☎ 650-6900

Amato Opera, 37. 319 Bowery ☎ 228-8200

Apollo Theater, 2. 253 W 125th St ☎ 749-5838

Beacon Theater, 11. 2124 Broadway ☎ 496-7070

Cami Hall, 19. 165 W 57th St ☎ 841-9650

Carnegie Hall, 20. 154 W 57th St ☎ 247-7800

Church of the Heavenly Rest, 8. 2 E 90th St ☎ 289-3400

City Center, 21. 131 W 55th St ☎ 581-1212

Dance Theatre Workshop, 32. 219 W 19th St ☎ 924-0077

DiCapo Opera Theater, 12. 184 E 76th St ☎ 288-9438

Dixon Place at Vineyard 26, 28. 309 E 26th St ☎ 532-1546

Florence Gould Hall, 18. 55 E 59th St ☎ 355-6160

Frick Museum, 13. 1 E 70th St ☎ 288-0700

Guggenheim Museum, 9. 1071 Fifth Ave ☎ 423-3587

Haft Auditorium, F.I.T., 29. 227 W 27th St ☎ 279-4200

Hammerstein Ballroom, 27. 311 W 34th St ☎ 564-4882

Joyce SoHo, 38. 155 Mercer St ☎ 334-7479

Joyce Theater, 31. 175 Eighth Ave ☎ 242-0800

Juilliard Theatre, 15. 155 W 65th St ☎ 769-7406

Kaye Playhouse, 14. 695 Park Ave ☎ 772-4448

The Kitchen, 30. 512 W 19th St ☎ 255-5793

La MaMa ETC, 36. 74A E 4th St ☎ 475-7710

Lincoln Center, 16.
Broadway & 64th St ☎ 875-5000
·Alice Tully Hall ☎ 875-5000
·Avery Fisher Hall ☎ 875-5030
·Clark Studio Theater ☎ 355-4172
·Metropolitan Opera ☎ 362-6000
·NY State Theater ☎ 870-5570

Madison Square Garden, 26. Seventh Ave & 32nd St ☎ 465-6741

Manhattan School of Music, 3. 120 Claremont Ave ☎ 749-2802

Merkin Concert Hall, 17. 129 W 67th St ☎ 362-8719

Metropolitan Museum, 10. 1000 Fifth Ave ☎ 570-3949

Miller Theater, 5. Columbia Univ, W 116th St ☎ 854-7799

92nd St Y, 7. 1395 Lexington Ave ☎ 996-1100

PS 122, 34. 150 First Ave ☎ 477-5288

Radio City Music Hall, 24. 1260 Sixth Ave ☎ 247-4777

Riverside Church, 4. 490 Riverside Dr ☎ 870-6784

St Bartholomew's Church, 23. 109 E 50th St ☎ 378-0200

St Mark's-in-the-Bowery, 33. Second Ave & 10th St ☎ 674-8194

St Peter's Church, 22. 619 Lexington Ave ☎ 935-2200

Symphony Space, 6. 2537 Broadway ☎ 864-5400

Town Hall, 25. 123 W 43rd St ☎ 840-2824

TriBeCa Performing Arts Center, 39. 199 Chambers St ☎ 346-8510

Washington Square Church, 35. 135 W 4th St ☎ 777-2528

Listed by Site Number

Listed Alphabetically

Ambassador, 9. 215 W 49th St
☎ 239-6200

American Place, 20. 111 W 46th St
☎ 840-2960

Belasco, 36. 111 W 44th St
☎ 239-6200

Booth, 31. 222 W 45th St ☎ 239-6200

Broadhurst, 34. 235 W 44th St
☎ 239-6200

Broadway, 3. 1681 Broadway
☎ 239-6200

Brooks Atkinson, 15. 256 W 47th St
☎ 719-4099

Circle in the Square, 8. 1633
Broadway ☎ 239-6200

Cort, 13. 138 W 48th St ☎ 239-6200

Douglas Fairbanks, 47.
432 W 42nd St ☎ 239-4321

Ensemble Studio Theatre, 2.
549 W 52nd St ☎ 247-3405

Ethel Barrymore, 14. 243 W 47th St
☎ 239-6200

Eugene O'Neill, 10. 230 W 49th St
☎ 239-6200

**Ford Center for the Performing Arts,
40.** 214 W 43rd St ☎ 307-4550

47th St, 16. 304 W 47th St
☎ 239-6200

Gershwin, 6. 222 W 51st St
☎ 307-4100

Golden, 28. 252 W 45th St
☎ 239-6200

Harold Clurman, 50. 412 W 42nd St
☎ 594-2370

Helen Hayes, 39. 240 W 44th St
☎ 307-4100

Imperial, 22. 249 W 45th St
☎ 239-6200

John Houseman, 45. 450 W 42nd St
☎ 967-9077

Judith Anderson, 48. 412 W 42nd St
☎ 564-7853

Kaufman, 44. 534 W 42nd St
☎ 563-1684

Lamb's, 37. 130 W 44th St
☎ 997-1780

Longacre, 11. 220 W 48th St
☎ 239-6200

Lunt-Fontanne, 18. 205 W 46th St
☎ 307-4100

Lyceum, 25. 149 W 45th St
☎ 239-6200

Majestic, 33. 247 W 44th St
☎ 239-6200

Marquis, 24. 211 W 45th St
☎ 307-4100

Martin Beck, 27. 302 W 45th St
☎ 239-6200

Minskoff, 32. 200 W 45th St
☎ 869-0550

Music Box, 23. 239 W 45th St
☎ 239-6200

Nat Horne, 46. Ninth Ave & 42nd St
☎ 279-4200

Nederlander, 53. 208 W 41st St
☎ 307-4100

Neil Simon, 5. 250 W 52nd St
☎ 307-4100

New Amsterdam, 41. 216 W 42nd St
☎ 307-4747

New Victory, 52. 209 W 42nd St
☎ 382-4000

Palace, 17. Broadway & 47th St
☎ 307-4100

Playwrights Horizons, 49.
416 W 42nd St ☎ 279-4200

Plymouth, 30. 236 W 45th St
☎ 239-6200

Primary Stages, 26. 354 W 45th St
☎ 333-4052

Richard Rogers, 21. 226 W 46th St
☎ 221-1211

Roundabout, 19. 1530 Broadway
☎ 719-1300

Royale, 29. 242 W 45th St
☎ 239-6200

St James, 38. 246 W 44th St
☎ 239-6200

Samuel Beckett, 51. 412 W 42nd St
☎ 307-4100

Shubert, 35. 225 W 44th St
☎ 239-6200

Signature Theater, 43.
555 W 42nd St ☎ 244-7529

Theatre Four, 1. 424 W 55th St
☎ 757-3900

Virginia, 4.
245 W 52nd St ☎ 239-6200

Walter Kerr, 12. 219 W 48th St
☎ 239-6200

Westside Theatre, 42.
407 W 43rd St ☎ 239-6200

Winter Garden, 7.
1634 Broadway ☎ 239-6200

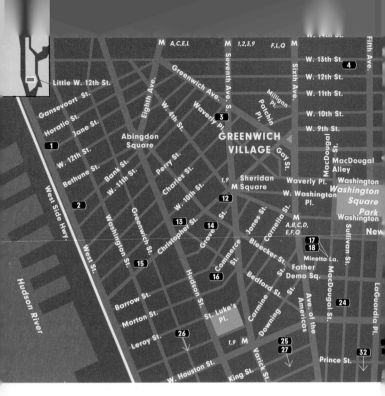

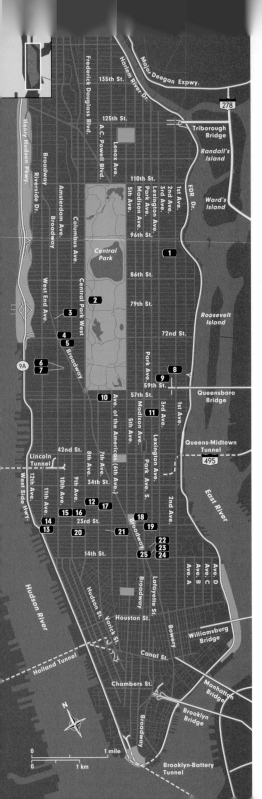

MAP 59 **Movies/Midtown & Uptown**

Listed Alphabetically

City Cinemas 1, 2, 3, 20.
Third Ave & 60th St
☎ 753-6022

City Cinemas Eastside Playhouse, 31.
919 Third Ave ☎ 755-3020

City Cinemas Murray Hill 34th St, 39.
160 E 34th St ☎ 689-6548

City Cinemas Sutton I & II, 26. Third
Ave & 57th St ☎ 759-1411

Clearview's Beekman, 14. 1254
Second Ave ☎ 737-2622

Clearview's Chelsea (1-9), 42.
260 W 23rd St ☎ 691-4744

Clearview's Chelsea West, 41.
333 W 23rd St ☎ 989-0060

Clearview's 59th St East Cinema, 22.
239 E 59th St ☎ 759-4630

**Clearview's First & 62nd Cinemas
(1-6), 21.** 400 E 62nd St ☎ 752-4600

Clearview's Metro Twin, 2.
Broadway & 99th St ☎ 222-1200

Clearview's Olympia Twin, 1.
Broadway & 107th St ☎ 865-8128

**Clearview's Park & 86th St
Cinemas, 6.** 125 E 86th St ☎ 534-1880

Clearview's 62nd & Broadway, 18.
Broadway & 62nd St ☎ 265-7466

Clearview's 34th St Showplace, 38.
Third Ave & 34th St ☎ 532-5544

Clearview's Ziegfeld Theatre, 27.
141 W 54th St ☎ 765-7600

Crown Gotham Cinema, 25.
969 Third Ave ☎ 759-2262

Donnell Media Center, 30.
20 W 53rd St ☎ 621-0624

East 86th St City Cinemas, 8.
210 E 86th St ☎ 860-8686

French Institute, 19.
55 E 59th St ☎ 355-6160

Guggenheim Museum, 5.
1071 Fifth Ave ☎ 423-3587

Loews 42nd St E Walk, 33.
8th Ave & 42nd St ☎ 505-6397

Lincoln Plaza Cinemas (1-6), 17.
B'way & 63rd St ☎ 757-2280

Loews Astor Plaza, 35. Broadway &
44th St ☎ 869-8340

Loews Cineplex Coronet, 24.
993 Third Ave ☎ 355-1664

Loews Cineplex State Theater, 34.
Broadway & 45th St ☎ 391-2900

Loews 84th St, 4. 2310 Broadway
☎ 877-3600

Loews Kips Bay, 40.
550 Second Ave ☎ 447-0638

Loews NY Twin, 13.
1271 Second Ave ☎ 744-7339

Loews Orpheum VIII, 7. 1538 Third
Ave ☎ 876-2400

Loews 72nd St East, 12. Third Ave &
72nd St ☎ 879-1313

Museum of Modern Art, 29.
11 W 53rd ☎ 708-9480

Naturemax, 10. American Museum of
Natural History, Central Park W & 80th
St ☎ 769-5650

Paris, 23. 4 W 58th St ☎ 688-3800

Sony Lincoln Square (1-13), 11. 1992
Broadway ☎ 336-5000

Symphony Space, 3.
Broadway & 95th St ☎ 864-5400

**United Artist Criterion Center
(1-7), 36.** 1514 Broadway ☎ 354-0900

United Artist East, 9. First Ave &
85th St ☎ 249-5100

United Artist 64th Street, 15.
Second Ave and 64th St ☎ 832-1670

Walter Reade Theater, 16.
165 W 65th St ☎ 875-5600

Worldwide Cinemas (1-6), 28.
340 W 50th St ☎ 246-1583

YWCA Cineclub, 32.
610 Lexington Ave ☎ 735-9717

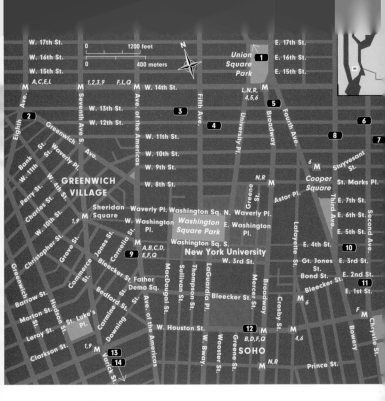

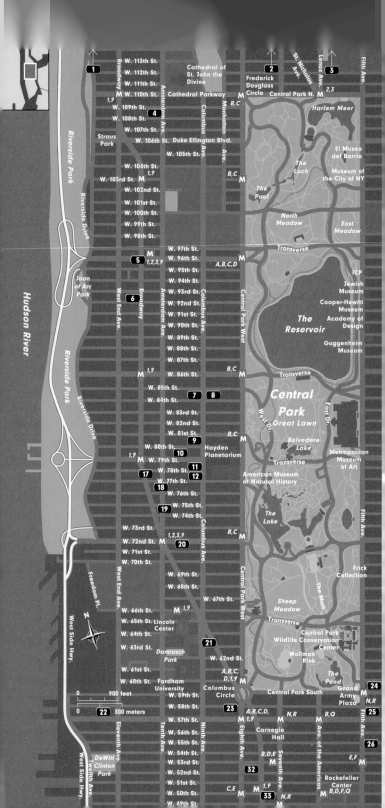

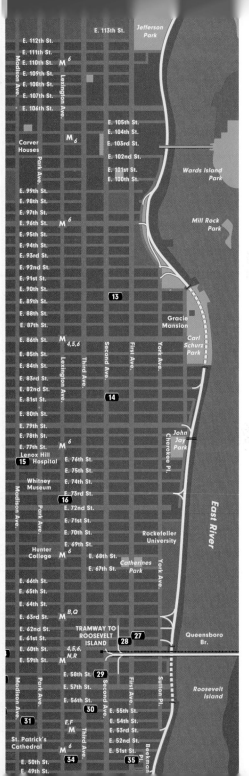

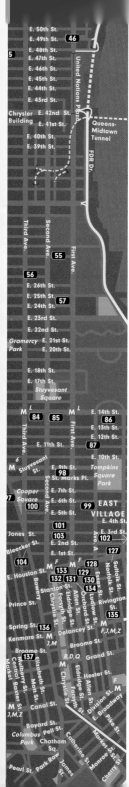

Listed Alphabetically

Algonquin, 47. 59 W44th St
☎ 840-6800. Cabaret

Arlene Grocery, 131. 95 Stanton St
☎ 358-1633. Rock

Axis, 67. 17 W 19st St
☎ None. Gay/Dance Club

Back Fence, 119. 155 Bleecker St
☎ 475-9221. Rock/Folk

Baggot Inn, 116. 82 W 3rd St
☎ 477-0622. Eclectic

The Bank, 128. 225 E Houston St
☎ 505-5033. Dance Club

Barmacy, 86. 538 E 14th St
☎ 228-2240. Bar

Barracuda, 64. 275 W 22nd St
☎ 645-8613. Gay

Beauty Bar, 84. 231 E 14th St
☎ 539-1389. Bar/Club

Beekman Bar and Books, 35.
889 First Ave ☎ 980-9314. Jazz

Bemelman's Bar/Café Carlyle, 15.
35 E 76th St ☎ 744-1600. Cabaret

Birdland, 51. 315 W 44th St
☎ 581-3080. Jazz

Bitter End, 118. 147 Bleecker St
☎ 673-7030. Jazz/Blues/R&B

Blue Note, 113. 131 W 3rd St
☎ 475-8592. Jazz/Blues/R&B

The Boiler Room, 101. 86 E 4th St
☎ 254-7536. Gay

Boston Comedy Club, 116.
82 W 3rd St ☎ 477-1000. Comedy

Bottom Line, 106. 15 W 4th St
☎ 228-6300. Folk/Rock

Bowery Ballroom, 136. 6 Delancey St
☎ 533-2111. Rock

Bowlmor Lanes, 82. 110 University Pl
☎ 255-8188. Bowling

Brownies, 87. 169 Avenue A
☎ 420-8392. Rock

Bubble Lounge, 146. 228 W
Broadway ☎ 431-3433. Champagne
Bar

Café Pierre, 24. 2 E 61st St
☎ 940-8185. Cabaret

Café Wha, 115. 115 MacDougal St
☎ 254-3706. Comedy/Jazz

Cajun, 75. 129 Eighth Ave
☎ 691-6174. Jazz

Caroline's, 33. 1626 Broadway
☎ 757-4100. Comedy

CBGB & OMFUG, 104. 315 Bowery
☎ 982-4052. Punk/Rock/Dance

Cheetah, 68. 12 W 21st St
☎ 206-7770. Dance Club

Chelsea Commons, 61. 242 10th Ave
☎ 929-9424. Bar

Chicago Blues, 79. 73 Eighth Ave
☎ 924-9755. Blues/Jazz

Chicago City Limits, 28. 1105 First
Ave ☎ 888-5233. Comedy

China Club, 42. 268 W 47th St
☎ 398-3800. Rock/Dance Club

Chumley's, 108. 86 Bedford St
☎ 675-4449. Bar

Cleopatra's Needle, 6. 2485
Broadway ☎ 420-8392. Rock

Comedy Cellar, 114. 117 MacDougal
St ☎ 254-3480. Comedy

Comic Strip, 14. 1568 Second Ave
☎ 861-9386. Comedy

Connolly's, 44. 14 E 47th St
☎ 867-3767. Irish

Continental, 100. 25 Third Ave
☎ 529-6924. Rock Club

Cooler, 78. 416 W 14th St
☎ 229-0785.

Copacabana, 22. 617 W 57th St
☎ 582-2672. Dance Club

Cornelia Street Cafe, 111.
29 Cornelia St ☎ 989-9318. Jazz

Cotton Club, 1. 125th St & West Side
Hwy ☎ 663-7980. Swing/Jazz

Cubby Hole, 83. 281 W 12th St
☎ 243-9041. Lesbian

Dangerfield's, 27. 1118 First Ave
☎ 593-1650. Comedy

Danny's Skylight Room, 38. 346 W
46th St ☎ 265-8130. Cabaret

Don Hill's, 143. 511 Greenwich Ave.
☎ 219-2850. Dance Club

Don't Tell Mama, 41. 343 W 46th St
☎ 757-0788. Cabaret

Double Happiness, 137. 173 Mott St
☎ 941-1282. Bar/Lounge

Duplex, 95. 61 Christopher St
☎ 255-5438. Cabaret/Comedy

The Eagle, 62. 142 Eleventh Ave
☎ 691-8451. Gay/Leather

Ear Inn, 139. 326 Spring St
☎ 226-9060. Rock/Blues

Elbow Room, 122. 144 Bleecker St
☎ 979-8434. Folk

Evelyn Lounge, 11. 380 Columbus
Ave ☎ 724-2363. Jazz/Blues

5757, 25. 57 E 57th St
☎ 758-5700. Piano Bar

Firebird Cafe, 37. 363 W 46th St
☎ 586-0244. Cabaret

Flamingo East, 85. 219 Second Ave
☎ 533-2860. Rock/Funk

g, 73. 223 W 19th St ☎ 929-1083. Gay

Gotham Comedy Club, 66. 34 W
22nd St ☎ 367-9000. Comedy

Greatest Bar on Earth, 148. 1 World
Trade Ctr ☎ 524-7011. Bar

Hell, 93. 59 Gansevoort St
☎ 727-1666. Dance Club

Henrietta Hudson, 112. 438 Hudson
St ☎ 924-3347. Lesbian

Holiday Lounge, 98. 75 St Marks Pl
☎ 777-9637. Bar

Improvisation, 39. 346W 46th St
☎ 924-2966. Comedy

Internet Cafe, 103. 82 E 3rd St
☎ 614-0747. Jazz

Iridium, 21. 48 W 63rd St
☎ 582-2121. Jazz

Irving Plaza, 81. 17 Irving Place
☎ 777-6800. Swing/Rock

The Jazz Standard, 58. 116 E 27th St
☎ 576-2232. Jazz

Joe's Pub, 97. 425 Lafayette St
☎ 539-8777. Nightclub/Cabaret

Judy's Chelsea, 72. 169 Eighth Ave
☎ 929-5410. Cabaret

Kava Lounge, 92. 605 Hudson St
☎ 989-7504. Bar

Kavehaz, 142. 123 Mercer St
☎ 343-0612. Jazz

Kenny's Castaways, 130.
157 Bleecker St ☎ 473-9870. Rock

King Cole Bar, 26. St Regis Hotel, 2 E
55th St ☎ 753-4500. Bar

Knickerbocker, 96. 33 University Pl
☎ 228-8490. Jazz

Knitting Factory, 147. 74 Leonard St
☎ 219-3055. Rock/Jazz

Latin Quarter, 3. 2551 Broadway
☎ 864-7600. Latin

Laura Belle's, 49. 120 W 43rd St
☎ 819-1000. Dance/Supper Club

Lava, 69. 28 W 20th St
☎ 627-7867. Dance Club

Le Bar Bat, 23. 311 W 57th St
☎ 307-7228. Dance Club

Lenox Lounge, 3. 288 Lenox
Ave
☎ 427-0253. Jazz

Lexington Bar & Books, 16. 1020
Lexington Ave ☎ 717-3902. Jazz

Life, 123. 158 Bleecker St
☎ 420-1999. Dance Club

Lion's Den, 117. 214 Sullivan St
☎ 477-2782. Rock

Living Room, 132. 84 Stanton St
☎ 533-7235. Rock

**Louisiana Community Bar & Grill,
125.** 622 Broadway ☎ 460-9633.
Jazz/Swing

Luna Lounge, 130. 171 Ludlow St
☎ 260-2323. Rock

Meow Mix, 127. 269 Houston St
☎ 254-0688. Lesbian

Michael's Pub, 30. 211 E 55th St
☎ 758-2272. Piano Bar/Jazz

Monkey Bar, 31. 60 E 54th St
☎ 838-2600. Bar

The Monster, 107. 80 Grove St
☎ 924-3557. Gay/Disco

Mercury Lounge, 129.
217 E Houston St ☎ 260-4700. Rock

Mother, 77. 432 W 14th St
☎ 366-5680. Performance Art

Nell's, 80. 246 W 14th St
☎ 675-1567. Dance Club

New York Comedy Club, 57.
241 E 24th St ☎ 696-5233. Comedy

Nuyorican Poets Cafe, 102. 236 E
3rd St ☎ 505-8183. Spoken Word
Performance

NV/289 Lounge, 140. 289 Spring St
☎ 929-6868. DJ

Ohm, 65. 16 W 22nd St
☎ 229-2000. Dance Club

Old Town Bar, 70. 45 E 18th St
☎ 529-6732. Bar

One 51, 34. 151 E 50th St
☎ 753-1144. Dance/Supper Club

Ozone Bar and Lounge, 13.
1720 Second Ave ☎ 860-8950. Bar

Paddy Reilly's, 55. 519 Second Ave
☎ 686-1210. Irish

Potion Lounge, 12. 370 Columbus
Ave ☎ 721-4386. Nightclub

Prohibition, 7. 503 Columbus Ave
☎ 579-3100. Funk/Jazz

Pyramid, 101. 101 Avenue A
☎ 473-7184. Dance Club

Rebar, 76. Eighth Ave & 16th St
☎ 627-1680. Eclectic

Red Blazer Too, 54. 32 W 37th St
☎ 947-6428. Jazz/Blues/Swing